Raising Academic Standards:
A Guide to Learning Improvement

by Ruth Talbott Keimig

ASHE-ERIC/Higher Education Research Report No. 4, 1983

Prepared by

 ® Clearinghouse on Higher Education
The George Washington University

Published by

Association for the Study of Higher Education

Jonathan D. Fife,
Series Editor

Cite as:
Keimig, Ruth T. *Raising Academic Standards: A Guide to Learning Inprovement:* ASHE-ERIC Higher Education Research Report No. 4. Washington, D.C.: Association for the Study of Higher Education, 1983.

The ERIC Clearinghouse on Higher Education invites individuals to submit proposals for writing monographs for the Higher Education Research Report series. Proposals must include:
1. A detailed manuscript proposal of not more than five pages.
2. A 75-word summary to be used by several review committees for the initial screening and rating of each proposal.
3. A vita.
4. A writing sample.

ISSN 0737-1292
ISBN 0-913317-03-9

ERIC° Clearinghouse on Higher Education
The George Washington University
One Dupont Circle, Suite 630
Washington, D.C. 20036

Association for the Study of Higher Education
One Dupont Circle, Suite 630
Washington, D.C. 20036

 This publication was prepared with funding from the National Institute of Education. U.S. Department of Education, under contract no. 400-82-0011. The opinions expressed in this report do not necessarily reflect the positions or policies of NIE or the Department.

CONTENTS

FOREWORD

"For higher learning, the most precious asset is public confidence. Despite constrained resources, higher education has, on the whole, managed to maintain the quality of its programs. But there are signs that quality standards are being jeopardized. Criticism is growing that many entering students are deficient in the academic skills necessary to successful pursuit of higher education, along with the subsequent suggestion that degrees no longer certify those who earn them are men and women of learning. These warning signs will be ignored only at great peril.

For this reason the Commission selected for its primary attention the issue of enhancing academic quality." (1982. p.r.)

This statement in the foreword of the National Commission's Report on Higher Education Issues entitled *To Strengthen Quality in Higher Education* (Washington, D.C.: American Council on Education) indicates the importance to higher education of establishing methods to raise or maintain their academic standards.

One solution that has been offered is to change admission standards so only the brightest are allowed entrance. The rationale is that if institutions admit students with academic deficiencies, then the quality of education will be lowered and the graduates will be *a priori* academically deficient. Not only is the assumption false—since it presumes once deficient, always deficient—it also ignores the historical mission of American higher education to provide educational opportunity to the largest number possible.

This "solution" assumes that the only recourse for a college or university is to lower standards rather than improve student performance.

The movement to raise admission standards has two other unacceptable results. First, it is indirectly racist, since a large majority of students demonstrating academic deficiencies are from minority groups. Second, it hinders the advancement of students who, through no fault of their own, have received an inferior education.

Since the establishment of Harvard in 1636, higher education has consistently been faced with admitting students who needed additional help to meet academic standards. In the 1800's, with the absence of a uniform high school system, institutions established preparatory units to help students move successfully into the regular academic program. Remedial os developmental education programs have served the same role today.

In this report by Ruth Talbott Keimig, formerly the Dean of Freshman and Chairman of the Learning Resources Division of Marymount College of Virginia and now a consultant in the area of adult education and training programs, these programs are reviewed. After carefully analyzing why many developmental programs have appeared to fail, Dr. Keimig develops a model that outlines the steps necessary to integrate learning improvement practices into the regular academic process. The greater the integration of learning improvement practices, the greater the reinforcement and consequently the increased probability of long term academic improvement.

Institutions can turn their backs neither on academic standards nor on countless students who have been a product of inferior schooling. Aside from the purely economic and survival reasons for many institutions to accept educationally disadvantaged students, there is still a need to fulfill the historical mission of U.S. higher education. The analysis in this report will greatly assist institutions in meeting their mission while still raising their academic standards.

Jonathan D. Fife
Director and Series Editor
ERIC° Clearinghouse on Higher Education
The George Washington University

ACKNOWLEDGMENTS

Ideas have their season, and the time is right for the Decision Guide for Effective Programs. Its development has been anticipated and influenced by many people with whom I have worked and studied.

From the George Washington University School of Education, I am indebted to Dr. Joseph A. Greenberg, for broad knowledge and experience enthusiastically shared; Dr. Ruth Peterson, teacher, friend, and professional colleague over the years; Dr. Martha Burns, who made valuable suggestions about organizing the data; Dr. Walter N. Davis, also of Prince William County (Virginia) Public Schools, for an extraordinary grasp of the management and organization of instruction.

The contributions should be noted of many individual faculty in undergraduate institutions, faculty who have participated with me in learning improvement and who have shared practical insights that are undoubtedly reflected but impossible to identify throughout the Decision Guide. I especially appreciate the work of Elizabeth Messman, Coordinator of the Learning Resource Center of the Marymount College of Virginia, whose superb teaching and counseling enlarge our perception of the possible in education.

I am indebted also to Allen and Karen, for their thoughtful editing, criticism, and encouragement of the developing manuscript.

A study group in the mathematics of chemistry was just beginning, being led by one of our student counselors, who said, "As you all know, 100 percent means one—the whole thing. . . ."

"That *is not* common knowledge," interrupted an older student, with firmness and dignity. "I just learned it yesterday."

A Student Counselor in
a College Learning
Assistance Center.

Curricular reform of significance requires (1) overall thought but (2) piecemeal action. Overall thought tends to lead to attempts at overall action, but overall action tends to lead to overall resistance. Piecemeal action tends to follow piecemeal thought. The difficult task is to get overall thought and then to have the patience and the persistence to carry out its conclusions one at a time. . . .

President Lowell of
Harvard University,
quoted in *Missions of
the College Curriculum*.

EXECUTIVE SUMMARY

Making Decisions in an Imperfect World

Most educators make decisions that directly affect students' learning and retention. Whether as faculty, administrator, program manager, student services coordinator, or specialist, an educator's daily decisions have cumulative effects, for good or bad, that may not be readily and immediately discernible. Yet a choice must be made, usually among alternatives that are poorly defined, shadowed by uncertainties beyond any one person's control, and constrained to a less-than-ideal set of possibilities.

So what's new? Haven't educational decisions always been difficult?

The demographic depression and the prevailing mood of decline, diminished resources, and threatened retrenchment are new, at least to this generation of faculty. So are the kinds of students new to the many institutions that have altered their admissions practices and curricula, as most institutions have done (Cross 1981; Carnegie Council 1980). Suppose too many students just drop the course, or transfer, or choose a different program with fewer and easier requirements? Compelled to choose between academic quality and retention, given today's underprepared mix of students, many educators make compromising and regrettable decisions. Abuses of integrity in the conduct of education are widespread (Carnegie Council 1979, 1980; Levine 1980). Colleges and universities are maintaining enrollments by retaining whatever students they have, by recruiting more aggressively, by reducing admissions standards, and by allowing students to finesse their way around requirements (Cross 1979; Manzo 1979).

College and Universities are maintaining enrollments by retaining whatever students they have.

Does it matter what students learn?

Students report cynicism about their academic "achievements" (Levine 1980, p. 66; Wellborn 1980). Faculty are not prepared to cope with the extreme diversity of students in their courses (Simmons et al. 1979; Cross 1976) and resent the circumstances they are forced to endure in today's educational environment. The public is losing confidence in and consequently diminishing support for higher education; that loss will rival the loss in prestige suffered by higher education during the 1960s era of student activism if integrity is not restored to the educational process (Carnegie Council 1980).

Improving the quality of learning for admitted students is basic to raising academic standards, because no other way exists for our current students to succeed by academically honest criteria in sufficient numbers to ensure the survival of our institutions and our programs. The improvement of instruction is the most urgent need in colleges and universities today (Carnegie Council 1979, 1980; Carnegie Foundation 1977; Levine 1980).

Do learning improvement programs make a difference in the achievement of postsecondary students?

Learning improvement programs have been the mainstay of higher education's response to its changing and underprepared student clientele. Whether designed to eradicate educational deficiencies (remedial) or to intervene with an appropriate learning experience at the time the need is recognized (developmental), since the 1960s the expected payoff from these programs has been increased grade point average (GPA) and retention. Remedial/developmental programs continue to be established in colleges and universities at a rate faster than any other type of course (Magarrell 1981, p. 1).

Learning improvement programs, however, have had mixed reviews in higher education (Richardson et al. 1981; Grant and Hoeber 1978; Roueche and Snow 1977; Cross 1976; Gordon 1975). The ambiguity of published assessments has its counterpoint in equivocal attitudes among faculty, who often regard developmental teaching as a mystery ("What can you *do* with these students?"), a lifeline ("You must do *something!*"), and a failure ("He has had English 099 and *still* can't answer an essay question.").

Using Research to Improve Learning and Retention

Knowing what really has worked to improve postsecondary achievement has been made more difficult by certain common but fallacious research practices. In many studies, (1) data about GPA and retention are inappropriately used to assess the effect of students' participation in a single remedial course; (2) quantitative outcomes from very different kinds of programs are averaged and statistically manipulated to provide general conclusions about the effectiveness of learning improvement programs, as though the qualitative differences among the programs and studies are unimportant; (3) the lack of a consistent framework of terminology about the goals, methods, structure, and evaluation of learning improvement programs interferes with comparing, understanding, and applying research results; and (4) important realities remain obscured and all effects are mistakenly attributed solely to whatever remedial/developmental service is being evaluated because program evaluators usually exclude relevant institutional factors from the analyses of causes and effects.

Despite the limitation of some research studies, what practical knowledge can be obtained from the literature?
A productive focus for action-oriented research is the qualitative analysis of successful programs to identify those specific practices that researchers have singled out as having positively contributed to improved GPA and retention. Researchers who have studied the effects on GPA and retention of many different learning improvement programs have much to say to the on-line educator about what works and what does not work to improve learning in college. Unfortunately, this extensive and important body of knowledge, derived from over 20 years of collective experience with postsecondary learning improvement, is generally inaccessible to academic faculty, administrators, and other decision makers who are oriented primarily to their own disciplines. Yet the findings and conclusions from these studies provide a base of practical, tested knowledge that could guide faculty and planners to those practices that have a record of having produced better learning.

In successful learning improvement programs, what characteristics are associated with increased GPA and retention?
Successful learning improvement programs are broadly described as having two dimensions: comprehensiveness and institutionalization.

Individualized support services are provided with the flexibility to meet a wide range of students' needs. Curricula are adjusted in the planning of academic courses and tutorial assistance, remediation, and ongoing social and psychological support provided.

In a successful program, the developmental concept is perceived as an institutional mission, and learning services are integrated into the academic mainstream. The remedial/developmental program has departmental or divisional status and maintains a close working relationship with the academic areas of the college or university.

Less successful programs emphasize remedial courses and precollege treatments, providing no systematic support services in academic courses. Operating as an appendage outside the college mainstream, less successful programs fail to effect the long-term changes in the institution's and in students' behavior through which lasting gains in GPA and persistence are made.

The Decision Guide for Effective Programs

Based upon a qualitative analysis of proven successful practices, the Decision Guide for Effective Programs summarizes the knowledge that pragmatic educators need to make informed decisions. The types and characteristics of postsecondary learning improvement programs are classified and ranked for their effectiveness in increasing GPA and retention. The analysis and data provide a consistent, logical basis for comparing programs on their essential elements and for selecting beneficial practices, despite the distraction of local, superficial differences in labeling or implementation.

What types of learning improvement programs are generally used?

In the Hierarchy of Learning Improvement Programs, four basic program types are described and ranked, differentiated by the extent to which they are comprehensive in response to the various needs of students and institutionalized into the academic mainstream.

Most common and least effective are the Level I, isolated courses in remedial skills. In ascending order (for impact on GPA and retention) are programs that combine certain additional elements to the basic courses: Level II, learning assistance to individual students; Level III, course-related supplementary learning activities for some objectives; and Level IV, comprehensive learning systems in academic courses.

What program features and characteristics are associated with improved GPA and retention?

Twenty-six critical variables for learning improvement are presented in the Hierarchy of Decisions. The possible choices that educators can make for each variable are identified and ranked for effectiveness to increase overall academic achievement.

For convenience, the 26 variables are grouped within the Hierarchy of Decisions, as decisions relating to goals and rationale, instructional methods and content, institutional policies and standards, professional and paraprofessional staff and roles, and the evaluation of learning improvement programs. The importance of some of the specific variables may be surprising, however, because they are typically not purposefully managed. Poor decisions about unrecognized but important determinants of achievement, therefore, often undercut an institution's effectiveness.

Variables such as the perception of the institution's responsibility, the local rationale for learning services, and the prevailing attitude toward nontraditional students may seem intangible. Yet they have profound effects on students' achievement and are highly responsive to leadership within a college or university.

Variables such as the responsiveness to students, the development of prerequisite skills, and the course instructor's role may appear tradition-bound and resistant to change. Yet they are readily evolved when remedial/developmental program resources are aligned with academic program resources to achieve specific, targeted goals.

The proper management of variables such as the direction of students into appropriate courses and services, the enforcement of competencies in academic courses, and the use of systematic procedures for advisement restore greater control of educational processes and outcomes to the faculty. The necessity to compromise quality to maintain enrollment is thereby reduced.

Why is learning improvement inexorably bound to instructional change in today's postsecondary environment?
As demonstrated in countless studies, the integration of learning services into the ongoing academic life of the institution is clearly superior. Researchers and policy analysts have also reached a consensus for instructional change in colleges and universities. The consensus affirms that a level of learning appropriate for college disciplines is unattainable by most underprepared students through traditionally delivered college instruction, regardless of previous, isolated remedial experiences.

The potential of a particular decision to promote or inhibit change in the institution's academic programs is therefore an inherent value for ranking possible choices about policies and programs for improving learning. The involvement of other faculty, administrators, and counselors profoundly affects both the content of the learning services offered as well as their success by fostering not only remediation for prerequisite abilities but also facilitative adaptations in the presentation of the academic material. Gaps in background knowledge are bridged and inappropriate behaviors of learners are overcome within the academic setting so that genuine learning can occur.

This interaction among academic and developmental educators is the fundamental dynamic in successful learning improvement programs, producing gains in GPA and retention that cannot be delivered by remedial/developmental personnel working alone in remedial settings. In most colleges and universities today, an administration that constrains developmental educators to isolated roles consigns to itself and to the academic faculty the unpleasant tasks of negotiating precarious compromises of program integrity amid today's relentless pressures for survival.

Overall Thought for Piecemeal Action

Few educators enjoy the luxury of starting over or the freedom to single-handedly execute sweeping changes in existing programs. Yet through their decisions, faculty and administrators control enormous resources that can be coordinated to produce greater control of learning outcomes than is commonly perceived. Educators need to know what specific activities and changes would be likely to improve learning, how to begin making the transition to more effective instruction, and how to focus resources on high-priority objectives.

Educators who use the Decision Guide achieve greater control of educational processes and outcomes through the use of more effective techniques of management, delivery, and evaluation. The use of the Decision Guide ensures the consideration of a full range of options and leads to the recognition of the possibilities available in an institution through the integration of existing resources, which are typically fragmented and underused. Planners of instruction and student services find within the Decision Guide the best methods for bringing students to acceptable standards of achievement. The use of the Decision Guide fosters long-term planning, interdisciplinary innovation, and evolutionary change to more effective programs even as short-term constraints force an immediate continuation of less desirable alternatives.

"Overall thought tends to lead to attempts at overall action, but overall action tends to lead to overall resistance. Piecemeal action tends to follow piecemeal thought," wrote Harvard president Lowell in 1938. "The difficult task is to get overall thought and then to have the patience and the persistence to carry out its conclusions one at a time . . ." (Carnegie Foundation 1977, p. 16). The Decision Guide for Effective Programs provides research-based overall thought to guide the pragmatic educator's piecemeal actions through which instructional programs and change can be evolved.

KNOWING WHAT WORKS TO IMPROVE LEARNING

To be useful in the decisions of busy educators, research results must be easily accessible, consistent, and relevant to their most pressing, practical concerns. The research literature on learning improvement programs, however, seems anything but practical and coherent to the practitioner who reads an occasional study, hoping to find a logical basis for decisions about instruction and student services. It is difficult to know what findings would be worthwhile in one's own situation because of the confusing differences among programs and studies, the imprecise and nonstandard terminology, and the sometimes contradictory outcomes that seem so typical of the literature. Despite the obvious importance of knowing how to improve students' academic performance, the vast amount of knowledge that has been accrued from more than 20 years of collective experience remains hidden and fragmented.

What is needed to make sense of this literature is a common and consistent framework of definitions, values, and criteria. Such a framework would provide a consistent method of analyzing students' learning needs and outcomes in their colleges as well as a basis for comparing the findings of various research studies (Richardson et al. 1981; Walvekar 1981).

Without such a framework for analyzing the data, the outcomes of learning improvement programs seem inconsistent and contradictory. Although many studies report positive effects on grade point average, the reported gains are often slight. Both negative and inconclusive reports are common, and a definitive assessment of the outcomes of learning improvement is not considered possible at this time (Richardson et al. 1981; Roueche and Snow 1977; Sherman and Tinto 1975). Long-term effects are rarely examined and are more likely to be equivocal than short-term effects, which are more likely to be positive (Trillin and Associates 1980).

What has gone wrong? Surely learning improvement programs should make a noticeable difference in the overall college performance of the students who are served. Increasingly, the value sought by most colleges when they establish remedial/developmental programs is improved learning and retention (Richardson et al. 1981; Maxwell 1979; Donnovan 1977; Fincher 1975; Pedrini and Pedrini 1970). The widespread use of inappropriate research designs for program evaluation, however, has tended both to depress the outcomes demonstrated and to obscure the relative strengths and weaknesses of very different programs and practices.

Misleading Assumptions

Implicit assumptions—which limit the real learning payoff and the demonstrability of positive outcomes—go unstated and unexamined in the design of many learning improvement programs and their evaluations. It is assumed that the "regular" academic program is a consistent criterion; that the "regular" program represents genuine, measurable learning; that the skills being developed through remediation are useful or necessary in other courses; that one instructor (remedial) should be held accountable for failures that occur in other ("regular") courses; that students should, can, or will choose to change their behavior permanently as a result of taking one remedial course. The evidence does not support these assumptions.

Assumption: A remedial course can have a measurable effect on GPA

Many programs and studies are constructed in the belief that a single variable, such as a characteristic of students (for example, reading ability or the participation in a precollege course), can be demonstrated statistically to influence GPA and retention.

The evidence

GPA and retention are complex outcomes with a large number of contributing factors (Carney and Geis 1981). Because educational variables tend to be interrelated, attempts to control or isolate them are usually unproductive (Donnovan 1977; Stufflebeam 1971). No single factor universally and unambiguously makes a difference in learning (Grant and Hoeber 1978). It seems reasonable to conclude that, when GPA and retention outcomes are used, any study that is narrowly focused on a few closely related independent variables—as are so many studies of remedial/developmental programs—can demonstrate only slight effects.

Assumption: The distinctions between remediation and college level work are based upon true differences

The prevailing myths of remediation (Maxwell 1979; Chaplin 1977b) and of "college level work" foster the attitude, "They should have learned *that* in high school." As a consequence, remedial teaching tends to be isolated from the academic mainstream in special programs in which a separate remedial faculty

What is needed to make sense of this literature is a common and consistent framework of definitions, values and criteria.

work toward the elimination of students' "deficits." If, later on, these students falter in the "real" academic world of other courses, the failures are cited as evidence of the ineffectiveness of the remedial program.

The evidence

Throughout the history of higher education in the United States and even today, agreement has never been reached on what constitutes "college level" instruction. The Carnegie Foundation addressed this issue in a chapter entitled "Basic Skills— Where Does College Begin?" (1977, chap. 11). The practice of adapting college instruction to the needs of its students has been the norm and the tradition in this country (Maxwell 1979; Cross 1976). Because of the double standard in research, whose focus has been primarily remedial/developmental programs, traditional methods and courses of instruction tend to continue, unexamined for effectiveness and unresponsive to whatever student needs are revealed in the evaluations of the remedial/developmental programs (Richardson et al. 1981; Donnovan 1977).

Assumption: GPA reflects learning

GPA is assumed to be a measure of how much students have learned.

The evidence

A strong tradition against evaluation, and resistance to it, exists in higher education; systematic analysis of the teaching/learning process and its outcome, student achievement, is seldom undertaken (Webb 1977). Once installed, programs tend to stay (Ball 1977). When programs are evaluated, they generally are poorly done (Grant and Hoeber 1978; Sherman and Tinto 1975). In all but a few institutions with competency-based programs, credit hours completed is the significant statistic for determining success and the completion of requirements.

Assumption: Student assessment equals program evaluation

Many practitioners consider student assessment synonymous with program evaluation (Richardson et al. 1981; Grant and Hoeber 1978). As a consequence, evaluators gather too much microscopic data (about individual students and classes) and do not consider enough macroscopic data (about relevant but possibly less easily quantified factors, such as the college, state, and national aspects of the problem being investigated) (Stuffle-beam 1971).

The evidence

The knowledge that measurement can provide is limited. The traditional indices of change, such as opinion surveys, test scores, and GPA, offer insights but never illuminate enough (Donnovan 1977). The "soft" data are necessary and acceptable evidence in program evaluations. Soft data include evidence based on observation/testimony, clinical/case study, systematic expert judgment, and survey analysis, whereas "hard" data include standardized student assessment, correlational status, and controlled experimental evidence (Ball 1977; Maxwell 1979).

Using Research to Make Better Program Decisions

Despite the ambiguities of published assessments, expectations persist that remedial/developmental programs can improve students' performance in the overall college program (Richardson et al. 1981; Magarrell 1981). The continued willingness of college administrators to invest in remedial/developmental programs and the persistence of positive outcomes with regard to GPA and retention in some careful, published studies despite the inadequacies, unknowns, and obstacles to good research may be testimony to the redemptive power of these programs in the colleges they serve (Roueche and Snow 1977). On the other hand, the persistence of positive statistics on GPA and retention may also reflect an institution's or curriculum's symbiotic adaptation through grade inflation and lowered standards to the students it has, without whom there would be no program. College planners need to know what is occurring in their institutions and need to effect positive control on the processes of change.

Decision makers need to know the answers to several questions: Do certain kinds of learning improvement programs affect the overall learning of students differently? Are these differences masked in summaries of the conclusions that combine the results of very different kinds of programs? Which decisions within a college directly affect students' academic performance? For the educator seeking to maximize the payoff (in academic performance and persistence) from investment in remedial/developmental programs, what intermediate outcomes—for the institution as well as its students—should be sought?

Given today's environment for higher education and the widely expressed mandate to improve postsecondary instruction (Cole 1982; Newton 1982; McCabe 1981; Levine 1980; Carnegie Council 1979, 1980; Carnegie Foundation 1977; Trillin and Associates 1980; Cross 1976, 1979; Maxwell 1979; Roueche and Snow 1977), the central issue becomes, What constitutes improved instruction? Which "basic processes" within the institution should be the subject of evaluation and possible reform when the goal is to improve students' retention and GPA?

"Better instruction" in today's educational environment is that which would enable contemporary students to learn and faculty to cope with the prevailing realities in ways that do not dilute the academic content of their courses and programs. Four specific circumstances inhibit learning yet are contemporary realities that educators must accommodate: a decline in basic skills, a shift in power, a willingness to cheat, and an intense competition for students.

Many and in some institutions most entering college students do not comprehend, write, compute, think analytically, or solve problems adequately for college study (Watkins 1981; Roueche 1981–82; Levine 1980, p. 72; Maxwell 1979; *Newsweek* 1975). The decline in basic skills affects all levels of ability and socioeconomic classes of students and cannot be attributed solely to shifts in the population of students entering college (Carnegie Foundation 1977, pp. 212–13). However, population shifts also are reflected in the changing nature of students (Cross 1981; Carnegie Council 1980).

In these economic hard times, faculty and institutions have lost power in relationship to students (Levine 1980). Even the most fundamental policies that every course instructor expects to control—grading practices, the acceptable quality and number of assignments, rules for attendance—tend to become negotiable currencies in daily confrontations between students and instructors (Cross 1979; Carnegie Foundation 1977; Manzo 1979). And on the average, students tend to win (Ashdown 1979).

Motivated largely by the desire to be able to get a job rather than by a quest for knowledge or by humanistic goals, many students cheat to get the grades they need—in all kinds of institutions, including the most prestigious and selective (Levine 1980, p. 66; Wellborn 1980, p. 39).

In the coming two decades, the proportion of students who are most diverse will increase, including students who are female, black, Hispanic, part-time, foreign, and concurrently enrolled in high school (Cross 1979, 1981; Carnegie Council 1980; Mayhew 1979). Institutions will compete harder to recruit, satisfy, and retain students, 40 percent of whom now drop out, boredom being cited most often as the reason for leaving (Carnegie Council 1980, p. 53).

Countless faculty-student-administrator transactions comprise the daily business of education, through which our changed students and circumstances are being accommodated. These daily transactions are the "basic processes" that must be understood and better managed to improve learning in today's higher education.

A Framework of Decisions That Affect
Learning and Retention

Context evaluation is the most basic type of evaluation, because it is concerned with providing a logical rationale for choosing educational objectives. Concerned with the total relevant environment, context evaluation describes the contrast between " . . . desired and actual conditions . . . ," identifies " . . . unmet needs and unused opportunities," diagnoses "the problems that prevent needs from being met and opportunities from being used . . . ," and provides an " . . . essential basis for developing objectives whose achievement results in program improvement" (Stufflebeam 1971, p. 218). Evaluations should account for a variety, not just a few, of student input variables, institutional variables, program variables, and outcomes (Roueche and Snow 1977, pp. 104–11).

Which aspects of the institutional context are relevant and important for improving learning and retention? Applying Stufflebeam's concept to the program planner's effort to increase students' success, the boundaries of the system being evaluated must include policies and practices in the "regular" program as well as practices of the remedial/developmental program. In the evaluation of a remedial/developmental program, the concurrent analysis of relevant features in the overall instructional programs and policies for freshmen would develop a basis for change within the total experience for freshmen. Better decisions about institutional and "regular" courses and about features of developmental programs would be likely to follow such an analysis.

The recurring daily decisions that educators make about instruction, programs, services, and policies comprise the context for learning in a college or university. Could a framework of these daily decisions be used to analyze institutional data and to clarify future possibilities and the desirable intermediate steps for improving learning? What are the critical decisions that affect how much students learn in today's colleges and universities?

Changing circumstances for higher education have produced a different institutional context and role for learning improvement programs. Old assumptions and methods are inadequate. New values and criteria are implicit in this changing context, and they call for new definitions of success for remedial/developmental programs.

How are the resources of learning improvement programs most effectively used within a college to improve students' overall learning and retention? Does research evidence support the continued use of separate skills courses to teach generic, basic skills that students can then transfer to other courses? Does evidence encourage the use of developmental program models that integrate developmental resources and activities into the regular academic courses?

Many research studies of the 1960s and 1970s were more broadly conceived and more comprehensive than the earlier and smaller studies had been. The comprehensive studies of those decades were better financed as well, because they were more often a central concern of college administrators themselves and were often undertaken to fulfill federal or state requirements (see Donnovan 1977; New York State Education Department 1977). The findings from such studies provide a vast store of practical information that is obscured by too much attention to terminal outcomes alone.

The focus in this analysis of the data is to identify program features that were associated with improved GPA and retention and then to determine what, if any, patterns emerge. The availability of many diverse and comprehensive studies has made this analysis possible, because the studies provide a considerable base of qualitative information about many different aspects of colleges' instructional practices, information that was excluded from earlier studies and is often overlooked in analyses that consider only outcomes related to GPA.

Characteristics of Successful Programs

When the success of remedial/developmental programs is measured by indicators of overall academic performance and persistence, the successful programs, despite many other differences, have certain characteristics in common. Although conclusive evidence is not available, successful programs have two broad characteristics in common: (1) comprehensiveness in their support services and (2) institutionalization of the developmental programs and goals into the academic mainstream.

Successful remedial/developmental programs offer comprehensive support services and have the flexibility to meet a wide variety of individual students' needs and to personalize the academic experience (Barshis 1979; Maxwell 1979; Donnovan 1977; Roueche and Snow 1977; New York State Education Department 1977, 1980; Cross 1976; Rossman, Astin, et al. 1975; Baehr 1969; Bridge 1970; Christensin 1971; Losak and Burns 1971; Smith 1972; Gordon 1975). Curricula are adjusted in the planning of academic courses, and tutorial support, remediation where necessary, and ongoing counseling and social and psychological support are provided (Renner 1979; Ludwig 1977; Jason et al. 1976; Gordon 1975; New York State Education Department 1977, 1980; Davis et al. 1973; McDill et al. 1969).

The individual is emphasized in a positive, person-centered environment that fosters self-concept (Barshis 1979; Roueche and Snow 1977; Donnovan 1977). Successful programs employ a developmental philosophy of instruction (Walvekar 1981, p. 21).

Successful programs are integrated into the academic and social mainstream, avoiding the punitive, low-status overtones and the ''you cure them'' mentality connoted by isolation within a separate remedial component (Maxwell 1979; Gordon and Wilkerson 1966; Donnovan 1977; Obler et al. 1977; Grant and Hoeber 1978; Fincher 1975; Sherman and Tinto 1975). In a successful program, the developmental program is institutionalized into the college and given the status of division or department (Grant and Hoeber 1978; Roueche and Snow 1977). The college administration thus demonstrates commitment to developmental goals and creates a highly visible testing ground for innovative efforts. The learning improvement program maintains a close working relationship with academic areas, a factor associated with success in four-year colleges (New York State Education Department 1980; Roueche and Snow 1977). In this way, all college support services can be coordinated. Comprehensive course designs that integrate the development

. . . successful programs have two broad characteristics in common: (1) comprehensiveness in their support services and (2) institutionalization . . . into the academic mainstream.

of basic skills into regular course content are associated with success (Renner 1979; Ludwig 1977; Carter 1970; Shaughnessy 1977; Bergman 1977; Fishman and Dugan 1976; Schiavone 1977).

The specific features of learning improvement programs (such as clearly articulated goal statements and systematic instruction) that various colleges use to achieve comprehensive student support and an institutionalized developmental philosophy of instruction are clearly very important. (The complete list of research-validated features is discussed in the following sections.) The composite result of whatever specific program features have been deployed, however, is an instructional program that meets a greater or a lesser number of students' needs and a developmental concept that is more or less institutionalized into the academic mainstream. It is these two dimensions, however they have been achieved, that make the difference in how much students learn. Colleges that meet a greater number of students' individual learning needs and integrate the developmental concept and practices into their overall academic program obtain better learning and retention outcomes for their students.

Characteristics of Less Successful Programs
Just as successful programs share certain characteristics, less effective programs, which fail to improve overall learning and persistence, have certain characteristics in common: an emphasis on remedial courses, a lack of systematic support services, and a lack of institutionalization.

Isolated remedial courses did not make a difference in students' overall success or retention and were the least effective of all remedial efforts (Berg and Axtell 1968; Klingelhofer and Hollander 1973; Bynum et al. 1972; Grant and Hoeber 1978). Traditional remedial courses seem "relatively ineffective" but are suitable for targeted remediation based on specific identified needs (Roueche and Snow 1977; Gordon 1975). Most students resent remedial courses; they perceive them as a rehash of earlier schooling and a delay for their other study (Fincher 1975). More of the same cannot and will not succeed (Shaughnessy 1977; Grant and Hoeber 1978).

The impressive gains often recorded in remedial courses do not seem to hold up past the semester including the course (Trillin and Associates 1980). Success in remedial course work does not readily transfer to traditional academic disciplines. Away from the remedial instructor's influence and back in the traditional academic environment, students revert to their old habits. Most attempts to change human behavior are suspect when subjected to rigorous analysis and evaluation (Fincher 1975).

For disadvantaged students, the hours of tutoring and counseling intervention are positively correlated with GPA (Brehman and McGowar 1976). When systematic support services are not available, students receive less tutoring and counseling. Learning improvement programs in which systematic support services are not used tend not to improve students' overall academic performance (Gordon 1975).

Remedial/developmental programs outside the academic mainstream are ineffective. They lack clear goals or have goals incompatible with the institution's goals, "in essence . . . neglecting to address the issue of systematically changing the structure of the institution" (Sherman and Tinto 1975, p. 15). Unsuccessful programs operate as appendages, without a theoretical base, separate from the institution (Gordon 1975; Fincher 1975).

Remedial/developmental programs are failing because they have not yet found the right solutions to the problems involved (Fincher 1975; Gordon and Wilkerson 1966). Practitioners in the field do not agree as to how, when, and where developmental efforts should be organized. The most common approaches to learning improvement programs are precollege summer programs, concurrent first semester programs, and "vestibule" or "holding" colleges where deficiencies must be corrected (Grant and Hoeber 1978, p. 19). These courses and programs are usually designed to prepare students for the inflexible, traditional curriculum. Institutions refuse to see them as an indication that the institution's entire curriculum may need revision (Newton 1982; Grant and Hoeber 1978).

Lacking an institutionwide developmental purpose and rationale, learning improvement programs fail to effect the long-term changes in the institution's responses and in students' behavior through which long-term gains in academic learning and persistence are made. The evaluation of students' achievements in less successful programs, focused narrowly on the practices of the isolated developmental program, does not develop the problem-solving dialogue with other program managers and faculty through which the institution's procedures might be changed, nor does it develop an institutional information base and theory of successful practice.

Making the Transition from Existing to Improved Programs

For students in college today, the Carnegie Council (1980) recommends (among others):

> . . . education that teaches the skills of reading, writing, arithmetic, speaking, problem solving, "crap detecting" (in identifying the drivel, exaggerations, and untruths that we hear and read each day). . . . These skills are critical for a generation raised on the media, weak in the three R's . . . (Levine 1980, p. 131).

The education thus described is not conceptualized as one in which basic and cognitive skills are assumed to have been developed before college; rather, they are developed within it and through it. Students' needs are thought of, not as individual deficiencies, but as acculturated characteristics developed in response to unfortunate and damaging circumstances of society. (See Levine 1980, chaps. 6 and 7, for an insightful discussion of contemporary society and its impact on young people.)

A basic principle in the design of instruction is to begin at a level consonant with students' backgrounds of already acquired prerequisite knowledge and skills. The affirmation of this principle in the proposals of recent policy commissions for higher education and in the research on learning improvement has enormous implications for the design of both academic and learning improvement programs for today's underprepared college population.

Yet existing programs, policies, and staffing cannot be discarded or reformed by decree. We must understand what decisions foster gradual change in regular college programs, how consensus for these changes can be achieved among an independent and traditional faculty who are oriented primarily to their own disciplines and who may not be informed about the methods or the urgency to improve learning, and what specific changes and activities have been demonstrated to promote learning. The Decision Guide for Effective Programs is a tool for the practitioner, an aid that provides accurate information about what works to improve learning and the most practical first steps toward achieving better instruction.

Possibilities are as important in the Decision Guide as the historical record of what has worked to improve learning. The comprehensive set of possible choices within each type of decision provides not only the ideal choice but also the effective intermediate and incremental choices that can be made until consensus for greater change is achieved. The annotated research findings that justify the ranking of choices provide a quick summary of the data as well as the reference where more detailed information can be obtained if it is desired. A very productive use of the Decision Guide is as a model for the collection and interpretation of in-house data, which can then be used to increase awareness of the need for learning improvement and to develop an institutional rationale and experiential basis for change.

Two inseparable values underlie the ranking of programs and possible decisions within the Decision Guide for Effective Programs: their demonstrated potential for improving learning in the overall academic program and their potential for bringing about gradual change toward the use of more responsive methods in academic courses. These rankings reflect the analyses and conclusions of countless diverse research studies in which GPA was a measured outcome. They also reflect the emerging consensus that traditional postsecondary instruction must change to promote genuine learning in today's higher education environment (Cole 1982; Newton 1982; McCabe 1981; Levine 1980; Carnegie Council 1979, 1980; Carnegie Foundation 1977; Trillin and Associates 1980; Cross 1976, 1979; Maxwell 1979; Roueche and Snow 1977).

The interdependence of these two values—improved learning and changed instruction—is the central message of the research literature. How to obtain these values in a college or university is the central message of the Decision Guide for Effective Programs. The Decision Guide is a plan for our time—a time when learning improvement is an urgent necessity, a time when improvements must come from the more effective use of existing resources rather than from major new initiatives.

The Hierarchy of Learning Improvement Programs

The organizational structure of the learning improvement program extends or limits its effect on achievement and retention more than any other single characteristic of the program. The mechanisms that operate to make this statement true and the four commonly used types of programs are described in Figure 1. The four types of programs are differentiated by the extent to which they provide comprehensive support services to meet a broad spectrum of students' personal learning needs and are institutionalized into the academic mainstream of the college or university. Within the Hierarchy of Learning Improvement Programs, the higher level programs include each of the lower level program structures plus additional features that achieve greater (1) comprehensiveness and (2) institutionalization.

Level I programs: Remedial courses

Separate remedial, basic skills courses are historically the most widely used structure for learning improvement programs. This program structure is based on two assumptions: (1) The student has a deficit (such as a lack of writing ability or a bad attitude)

Figure 1
The Hierarchy of Learning Improvement Programs

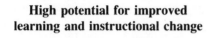

**High potential for improved
learning and instructional change**

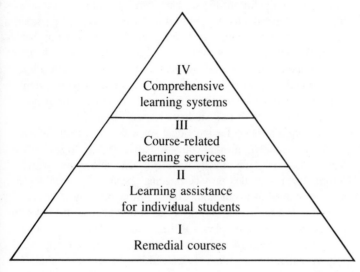

IV
Comprehensive
learning systems

III
Course-related
learning services

II
Learning assistance
for individual students

I
Remedial courses

Low

that interferes with college learning; when the deficit is overcome (in the remedial course), the student will succeed;
(2) Skills such as critical thinking, reading, problem solving,
and quantitative reasoning can be developed as generic skills in
separate courses; students will then transfer these new skills to
other applications in other courses.

Neither of these assumptions is supported by the research literature for the students who need remediation in college. It is
increasingly recognized that generalized approaches to remedial
and tutorial assistance are less likely to be effective than those
targeted at specific aspects of learning within the academic
courses in which the need for the knowledge or skill becomes
apparent (Gordon 1975).

Separate remedial, basic skills courses are at the lowest level
in the Hierarchy because they are the least likely to effect long-
term academic achievement and persistence and because they
tend not to foster the shared problem solving (with other fac-

ulty and counselors) that leads to providing improved and more responsive learning environments in the regular academic program.

Level II programs: Learning assistance for individual students
Learning assistance for individual students is based upon the assumptions that (1) the student has the problem and therefore must seek the solution; (2) students can overcome deficiencies through independent study and tutorial assistance; (3) personal attention helps to counter low self-esteem and poor study habits and will enable students to overcome academic failure. Learning assistance centers and various tutorial services came into widespread use in the 1960s and 1970s. Students who sought extra help could obtain it through a center; some tutorial programs assigned high-risk students to peer counselors.

Learning assistance for individual students offers many advantages over isolated remedial courses. The advantage to students is that they receive help directly with their academic course work, in informal situations that provide ongoing social and psychological support as well as instruction. Course instructors may refer students for assistance and may seek out developmental instructors to discuss the learning problems of their students. When these contacts occur, developmental program personnel have the opportunity to obtain firsthand knowledge and insight into institutional practices and problems, knowledge that can then be used to build support for more effective services.

Learning assistance for individual students comprises Level II of the Hierarchy of Learning Improvement Programs because, when established in addition to instruction in basic skills, the likelihood increases that some students' atypical needs will be met and their learning improved. Assistance to students with their academic course work is an important component of college learning improvement programs, because it can be a developmental planner's first step out of the narrow confines of a separate program toward more comprehensive and better coordinated services and the academic instructor's first step toward creating a more responsive classroom environment.

Learning assistance to individuals is not effective as a total program, however. Tutorial assistance to individuals, when it is the only service, is the least successful for students' overall success because it fails to address students' very real weaknesses in knowledge and skills (Cross 1976). Such informal or ''walk-in'' learning assistance has several major disadvantages:

(1) it is not systematic; (2) it tends to be used too little, too late; (3) it happens after a failure has occurred rather than earlier to prevent the failure (Grant and Hoeber 1978); and (4) it usually is avoided by the students who need it most.

Level III programs: Course-related learning services

Systematic coordination of developmental objectives and activities into academic course assignments distinguishes the Level III programs from the lower level programs. All the students within a given class or course have the opportunity to participate in the supplementary activities.

The assumption in Level III programs is that the college must provide whatever extra instruction is necessary to bridge the gap between students' skills and knowledge at entry and those required to master the course material. The principles of mastery learning may also be the underlying philosophy behind supplementary instructional opportunities to ensure that appropriate learning occurs. Students' learning needs are presented as being necessary because of the nature of the objectives and content of the course rather than because of students' deficiencies. Therefore, all students have access to supplementary, possibly innovative, instructional experiences, which benefit nonremedial students as well (Gordon 1975).

In a Level III program, adjunct learning experiences for review, reinforcement, and/or reteaching of selected requisite topics are integrated into the ongoing requirements for the course. Through a variety of assignments, including media, tutorial, and small-group learning experiences, students receive additional directed instructional time with important course content. They may have to demonstrate competency as well. Mastery learning technology, in which students practice and restudy until they demonstrate mastery, is particularly suited to Level III model programs. It is the most effective of the single developmental components for achieving academic success for the underprepared student (Cross 1976).

The trend in colleges is to replace traditional reading and study skills programs with learning centers. The learning center has three functions: service to students, training of teachers, and research and program development (Maxwell 1975). The feature that distinguishes Level III from Level II learning centers is the link of services to specific academic courses in Level III. Through this link, faculty receive help both for students with needs that faculty are ill-equipped to handle and with the

Systematic coordination of developmental objectives and activities into academic course assignment distinguishes the Level III programs from the lower programs.

extremes of diversity that have increased the instructor's workload (Cross 1976).

Lower level components have important roles in Level III programs. Lower level "walk-in" learning assistance leads to problem-solving interaction among students, academic faculty, and developmental personnel for learning objectives presently outside the course-related service. The learning assistance center thus becomes a laboratory for experimenting with more successful instruction (Manzo 1979) and a proving ground for innovations that can lead to more systematic and effective higher level services.

In a coordinated learning services program, the basic skills courses are designed to develop specific skills for a relatively smaller population of students, who are assigned to the courses on the basis of diagnostic placement tests. Skills courses are appropriate for the student whose needs are too pervasive to be met entirely in the course-related supplementary support components of the program. For example, students who need to relearn many operations in arithmetic should take the basic course, whereas students who need to review only percents can do so through learning experiences that are a part of the syllabus of a chemistry, nursing, or accounting course.

Level IV programs: Comprehensive learning systems
Different both in scope and precept from lower level programs, comprehensive learning systems provide for the total learning needs of all students through more sophisticated and complex methods than the reinforcement technology applied in Level III programs. Learning processes for the course or curriculum are purposefully designed with students' particular needs and attitudes in mind. The instructor does not merely dump information on an unknown student audience. Rather, the instructor uses a variety of resources and techniques to maximize students' involvement with the course and their commitment to learn.

In Level IV programs, the assumption is that the total educational experience within the course should be systematically designed according to the principles of learning theory. The student's overall developmental needs are provided for, including interpersonal and affective needs and cognitive and requisite skills. The instructor monitors students' responses (including learning) and adjusts teaching strategies and learning experiences individually.

The design of such instruction embodies several important concepts. Colleges can be educationally effective only if they reach students where they are, only if learning is made relevant to students' central concerns, and only if the three personal competencies (intellectual competence, physical-manual skills, and interpersonal competence) are developed as part of a whole (Chickering 1969). Time, rather than achievement, should be the variable in education. Students differ in the amount of time needed for learning; by increasing time spent on a task, students can learn a given content to specified criteria (Grant et al. 1979)

Developmental theorists such as Bruner, Erikson, and Piaget proposed hierarchical, cross-cultural, predetermined sequences in the growth or maturation of abilities. A "critical period" is the time when an individual is most ready for a "task-relevant experience" to help facilitate his or her development. "Intervention" with the appropriate learning experience at the critical time promotes maximal learning (Roueche and Snow 1977, p. 13). Other significant teaching methodologies include cognitive behavior modification (Killian 1980; Sadler and Whimbey 1979), inquiry teaching, problem solving (Whimbey and Lockhead 1981; Ozer 1980), Piagetian learning cycles (Killian 1980), and reading in the content areas.

A comprehensive, instructional system is synthesized out of conventional instructional practices and developmental learning theory, guided by the practical experience of what works best for given students in a particular course. A comprehensive system includes whatever content, personal growth, and learning activities students need to accomplish the objectives of a course, merged into a coherent and unified instructional program using personalized course and instructional support activities (Newton 1982, p. 42).

Comprehensive programs represent the highest level in the Hierarchy of Learning Improvement Programs because they are most likely to improve students' learning and to effect change in academic instruction. Comprehensive systems are best evolved out of the experiences derived from lower level programs for three reasons: (1) the lower level support components must be in place to provide auxiliary learning experiences for the courses; (2) the experience that developmental and regular instructors obtain in implementing lower level services provides planners with the knowledge and confidence they need to establish comprehensive systems; (3) continued, quiet, incremental change is more likely to occur and be accepted than massive reforms undertaken all at once (Levine 1978, p. 420).

Relatively few Level IV programs, compared to the number of remedial course programs, are described in the research literature. Early holistic attempts involved team teaching to achieve the fusion of instruction in reading/study skills into history/social studies courses and an engineering physics course (Diamond 1976; Shaw 1960). A recent structure is the back-to-back reading/content course, sometimes called "piggybacking." All students in an academic course are enrolled in the parallel reading course, in which text and course materials are used to develop mature reading abilities (Moran 1980; Bergman 1977).

"Block programs" at the Community College of Allegheny County (Pennsylvania) are multidisciplinary courses incorporating reasoning, reading, writing, speaking, or mathematics instruction into an academic course such as social studies, which meets for expanded hours of time (Holmberg et al. 1979).

The Loop College (Chicago) program is a holistic system of block courses and a full range of support services for individualizing instruction, including peer tutoring and audiovisual instruction (Barshis 1979).

At the University of New Mexico, freshmen below certain levels are placed in social studies or natural sciences courses of their choice designed primarily to raise students' ability to read, analyze, and evaluate the materials of the discipline. In these courses, the goal of developing generic cognitive skills is considered more important than learning content (Minnick and Teitelbaum 1980). An individualized social studies instructional program at Cuyahoga Community College (Ohio) has been successful in raising students' cognitive levels of operation in processing the content of the course (Ludwig 1977).

At Southern Illinois University, as part of the Acceleration Program in Science and Technology for disadvantaged students, the quasi-modular approach (QMA) is used for the teaching of remedial and precalculus mathematics. QMA is a comprehensive learning system that coordinates counseling and tutoring, with conventional lectures that have workshops built in. The early courses in the acceleration program comprise an alternative educational system founded on cognitive and affective support systems (Jason et al. 1976).

In practice, the distinction between Level III and Level IV programs blurs somewhat, because real programs often contain a mixture of elements from both levels. The Loop College program, for example, is totally a Level IV program, able to respond to the whole gamut of inner-city students' needs through a highly personalized system of support. QMA is also fully comprehensive for students' cognitive and emotional developmental needs; however, it is targeted only at mathematics. Other programs, such as those at the University of New Mexico and Cuyahoga Community College, apply learning theory and systematic course designs to achieve students' language and cognitive developmental needs (thereby qualifying as Level IV programs) but foster students' affective development only incidentally through procedures that may be more characteristic of Level II or Level III programs. The distinction between Level III and Level IV programs is important, however, because it provides a meaningful basis for classifying and comparing programs and for designing improved program elements.

The Hierarchies of Possible Decisions

Within an existing learning improvement program, whatever its structure, instructors and managers make many important decisions that will affect program outcomes. The possible decisions that can be made represent the options that managers can use to design services, procedures, policies, and other features of the program. However, these options may not exist in the institution and therefore may have to be created (Stufflebeam 1971), or less desirable decisions, already operationalized, may have to be changed. Decision makers need to know what variables in a learning improvement program are associated with improved academic achievement and what presently existing program features should be analyzed for effectiveness and possible modification.

Important program features

Certain variables (features) of learning improvement programs occur frequently in research studies and are repeatedly cited as being of central importance in determining the learning outcomes described in the studies. Although these variables are grouped for convenience around the usual categories of decisions that are made for any program—the goals and rationale, the methods and content, the policies and standards, the staff and roles, the evaluation process—many of the variables are neither widely recognized nor typically used to full advantage.

Figure 2 lists the variables that researchers have identified as being associated with improving learning. Decisions must be

Figure 2
Critical Variables for Learning Improvement Programs

- **Goals, Objectives, and Rationale for Instruction**
  1. Developmental program goals
  2. Perceptions of institutional responsibility
  3. Methods for choosing instructional objectives
  4. Rationale for learning services
  5. Compatibility of developmental goals with regular program and institutional goals
  6. Attitude toward nontraditional students
  7. Structure of the developmental program

- **Instructional Methods and Content**
  8. Methods of instruction
  9. Responsiveness to students
  10. Development of cognitive and basic skills
  11. Affective development of students
  12. Control for learners success

- **Institutional Policies and Standards**
  13. Directing students into appropriate courses and programs
  14. Definition of competencies in academic courses
  15. Credit earned for remedial developmental study
  16. Systematic procedures for advisement
  17. Organization of the developmental program within the college
  18. Institutionalization of developmental services

- **Professional and Paraprofessional Staff and Roles**
  19. Regular course instructor's role
  20. Developmental program staff and role
  21. Counseling staff and role
  22. Faculty and staff development

- **Evaluation of Learning Improvement Programs**
  23. Institutional context and outcomes
  24. Student outcomes
  25. Academic standards and the grade point average
  26. Ongoing evaluation

made about each of them. Therefore, these variables comprise a comprehensive list of the critical factors in the design of a remedial/developmental program. Decisions about these features distinguish various programs, are likely to affect their success, and therefore will be most productive as starting points for the analysis and redesign of a particular instructional program.

Ranking the possible options

In the Hierarchies of Possible Decisions, the decisions that can be made about each program variable are summarized and ranked according to their probability of effecting positive change in students' overall achievement and instruction within the college. In the aggregate, these decisions comprise a comprehensive list of the options from which educators can select the most facilitative combination of program features for a particular situation.

The four levels of alternative decisions for each variable provide general parameters rather than specifically defined alternatives for the choices available. Level IV decisions rank high on the Hierarchies because they enhance long-term overall learning and because they facilitate evolutionary instructional change; Level I alternatives rank low because they are least likely to obtain positive overall effects. The levels in between suggest increasingly desirable alternatives, as measured against the values of greater learning and change being sought from learning improvement programs today. The levels are intended to suggest a continuum of possible variation on the dimension being considered for decision rather than fixed, precisely defined limits.

The most comprehensive, institutionalized, ideal alternative for each decision would of course be the Level IV decision. However, it is usually not practical, prudent, or possible to attempt to initiate learning improvement programs with all Level IV options. In reality, a college learning improvement program usually includes activities and features from each level; support for one academic division may be course-related and systematic and for another may be on an unorganized walk-in basis only or nonexistent. It takes years of shared experiences within a college to know which practices should be institutionalized and to achieve consensus for doing so. Colleges should initiate new programs with primarily remedial components until institutional experience and knowledge lead to evolving more complex program features (New York State Education Department 1977).

An extensive body of research supports the values implicit in the Hierarchies and the relative superiority of certain program features over others for obtaining these values. Comprehensive studies have been made of multiple programs in which comparative analyses of program elements and effects have been obtained (see, for example, Simmons et al. 1979; Grant and Hoeber 1978; New York State Education Department 1977; Donnovan 1977; Roueche and Snow 1977). Researchers of individual programs have also specified elements associated with the success of a particular developmental program. Therefore, certain variables have been validated to be associated with students' long-term academic improvement and retention in a large number of two-year and four-year institutions; they are included in the Hierarchies.

Conclusive proofs are not available, however. Researchers have far more evidence about what does not work in the long term (isolated remediation) than proof of what does because of the past emphasis on remedial programs and the less frequent use of integrated, comprehensive ones. It may also be true that the best instructional systems have subsumed the developmental concept into a focus that is entirely on students' learning of the content (engineering, for example) and thus may not be recognizable as developmental programs (Simmons et al. 1979).

The Hierarchy of Decisions Relating to Goals, Objectives, and Rationale

Successful learning improvement programs are founded upon statements of rationale and goals that define the specific needs and problems that the learning improvement program should address as institutional missions. Instead of "You (the remedial/developmental staff) must solve these problems," the approach is, "Our students need these things. How can we best help them learn?" Local institutional data are interpreted in the light of the relevant general issues within today's higher education environment. Institutional concerns and problems are more understandable and fewer hackles are raised when it is apparent that nearly every college and university is struggling with the same problems. Local data and problems become the basis for dialogue among faculty, departments, and committees at all levels in the college. Through this dialogue, appropriate rationale, goals, and objectives are chosen—for academic programs as well as for the developmental program.

Figure 3 contains the decisions relating to goals, objectives, and rationale that researchers have identified as having impact on the success of learning improvement programs. The variables are:

1. developmental program goals
2. perceptions of institutional responsibility
3. methods for choosing instructional objectives
4. rationale for learning services
5. compatibility of developmental goals with regular program and institutional goals
6. attitude toward nontraditional students
7. structure of the developmental program.

Variable 1. Developmental program goals
Goals are imprecise, poorly thought out, and not specified in many programs, which as a consequence are haphazardly implemented and impossible to evaluate (Sherman and Tinto 1975). Goals should include both short-range and long-term student-centered, staff-centered, program-centered, and institutional outcomes (New York State Education Department 1977). Expectations for students may range from providing equal opportunity to providing a little better chance (Grant et al. 1979).

Level I decisions. Emphasizing the short-term goal of students' achieving readiness for college work (Minnick and Teitelbaum 1980), objectives for the remedial program concern the development of basic skills, playing "catch-up" (Webb 1977).

Level II decisions. Goals are established for individual students.

Level III decisions. Certain shared developmental and academic program objectives are specified to be accomplished in supplementary learning experiences, which are presented as part of the ongoing life of the course.

Level IV decisions. Comprehensive goals include all students, all learning encompassed by the course, and relevant staff and programmatic outcomes for both the developmental and regular programs. Long-term and short-term developmental program goals are established for students, staff, program, and instruction.

Variable 2. Perceptions of institutional responsibility
In the past, attention was given to creating conventional students out of disadvantaged ones. Now it is more generally perceived (as occasionally noted earlier—Gordon and Wilkerson 1966) that the more central problem is to reconstruct the educa-

Figure 3   The Hierarchy of Decisions:
                  Variables

Developmental Program Goals	Perceptions of Institutional Responsibility	Methods for Choosing Objectives
Include long- and short-term goals for academic and developmental programs, students, staff, and institution.	Accept that the college should adapt regular instruction to meet the needs of all admitted students.	Base choice on applied institutional research into learning status, course requirements, students' needs.
Include specific, course-related objectives.	Acknowledge the need to provide systematic support for some objectives only, in existing courses.	Base choice on systematic analysis of some class tests or work.
Include goals primarily for individual students.	Limit college's responsibility to making extra help available.	Teach standard developmental content or course material that student requests.
Specify goals in terms of students' general readiness for college work.	Perceive college's responsibility only to admit atypical students. Accept high attrition as inevitable.	Teach standard developmental content.

Possible Decisions

Potential for Improved Learning and Instructional Change

High →

Low ←

Relating to Goals, Objectives, and Rationale

Variables

Rationale for Learning Services	Compatibility of Goals	Attitude toward Students	Structure of Developmental Program
Focus program on possibilities and needs to know within curriculum unit.	Link developmental goals to college's mission statement. Use committees to negotiate developmental concept into other programs' goals.	Accept all admitted students nonjudgmentally, with positive expectations.	IV Comprehensive Learning Systems
Focus program on prerequisite objectives with known criteria for exit or competency.	Create awareness of program-specific needs; articulate developmental/academic program goals.	Accept some students as necessary to populate programs; upgrade their skills as needed.	III Course-related Learning Services
Base program on student's deficiencies or problems in academic courses.	Negotiate developmental objectives with individual students and faculty.	Let the student obtain help to solve his own problem.	II Individual Learning Assistance
Base program on students' deficiencies on basic skills tests.	Accept "remedial" status and goals in an unyielding traditional college.	Isolate unfit students until deficiencies are remediated.	I Remedial Courses

tional system so that college is a useful experience for most young people (Kendrick 1969). The responsibility of the college is to educate admitted students, whether qualified or not (Simmons et al. 1979). The university needs to redefine its role in society and its responsibility for the education of all students, whether or not they fit the traditional image (Gordon 1975). American education may be judged historically by its success in educating the disadvantaged (Fincher 1975).

Level I decisions. The college provides easy access with a standard remedial program and accepts very high attrition when (as is often the case) students do not make a successful transition to the regular program (Roueche and Snow 1977).

Level II decisions. The college defines its responsibility in terms of making extra help available to individual students.

Level III decisions. The college acknowledges its responsibility to provide developmental support for some objectives. Because it is always easier to add an extension than to restructure the mainstream educational experience (Gordon 1975), the support is supplementary though coordinated within the ongoing academic course. Leadership and resources are provided to develop consensus for more basic instructional change.

Level IV decisions. Leadership and resources are expended on comprehensive institutional and programmatic adaptations of the instructional program to meet the full range of students' needs.

Variable 3. Methods for choosing instructional objectives
Faculty are ill-equipped to deal with the diversity of students in their courses (Simmons et al. 1979; Cross 1976). Faculty must learn new methods of teaching, testing, and thinking (Grant et al. 1979). Developmental specialists have a special role in helping faculty develop new abilities (Grant and Hoeber 1978) and in providing information obtained through local institutional research projects about students' status and learning needs and about effective approaches (Maxwell 1975).

Level I decisions. Students are taught traditional college preparatory courses in isolated remedial settings.

Level II decisions. Students are helped individually with routinely assigned, possibly entirely inappropriate (for them), academic course work or with standard remedial work selected from traditional college preparatory courses.

Level III decisions. Based on systematic analysis of selected class tests or work, developmental support for some objectives is provided through the academic course. Insight about students' learning needs is used in planning subsequent instruction.

Level IV decisions. Comprehensive revisions to the course and curriculum are based on local research findings and provide a full range of appropriate learning activities to develop the content of the course. Textbooks are selected for understandability. (Fifty-eight percent of engineering faculty considered this factor important in the success of students, reported Simmons et al. in 1979.)

Variable 4. Rationale for learning services

An institution reveals its attitude toward students in the title it selects for its basic skills program. A choice of "remedial" (implying blame) versus "developmental" (implying learning sequences or stages) is an ideological issue. The remedial or "deficit" model posits blame on students for lacking certain knowledge or skills. It is negative and should be abandoned (Cross 1976; Sherman and Tinto 1975). The questions are, Who has failed, the student or the educational system? and Who should change? (Grant and Hoeber 1978).

Level I decisions. The remedial component is based on students' deficiencies on basic skills tests.

Level II decisions. Students' problems in courses are the focus of the learning assistance provided.

Level III decisions. A supplementary basic skills component focuses on specific objectives identified within a related course or within a follow-on unit or course. Known standards for achievement and recognizably important definitions of competency favor students' acceptance of the instruction (New York State Education Department 1977).

Level IV decisions. A philosophy of basic skills instruction is articulated. Skills are taught as needed and as they are relevant to the content of the course, not as they are identified as deficient in a single test or performance. The rationale that guides instruction is one of possibility, not deficiency (Chaplin 1977a). Written statements of the program's philosophy and objectives foster success (Roueche and Snow 1977).

Variable 5. Compatibility of developmental goals with regular program and institutional goals

Are the goals of learning improvement programs accepted by the administration? By other academic program managers? Does the college's mission statement reflect a developmental

Developmental specialists have a special role in helping faculty develop new abilities.

philosophy of teaching? Many value systems are involved (Stufflebeam 1971): institutional values such as survival, mission, growth; external values such as requirements for accreditation and integrity of disciplines; subsystem values such as priorities for programs and curricula; and private, personal values and prejudices. The institutional impact of an active, successful developmental program includes the shifting of more resources to "C" and "D" students, a redistribution of the faculty's labor so that more time is spent teaching basic skills. Some faculty resist these changes (Grant et al. 1979).

Level I decisions. Unyielding elitist tradition is at odds with developmental philosophy and forces the constraint of "remedial" status on the learning improvement program. Most of the college reading programs reported in the literature have yielded to this constraint, despite the widespread dissatisfaction of reading specialists with this role (Walter 1979; Chaplin 1977b; Carter 1970) and despite the strong theoretical base within the literature for reading instruction based on academic course materials and content.

Level II decisions. The faculty believe that students should not be spoon fed. Developmental staff help individual students and faculty as much as possible and use the knowledge gained from individual experiences to negotiate shared goals for more systematic instruction to meet recurring needs.

Level III decisions. Local institutional research findings are disseminated to increase faculty's and administrators' awareness of the need for instructional services and development. If an adjunct service is contemplated, the relevance and value of undeveloped, requisite basic skills to course content are demonstrated. If the shared developmental-academic goals are not wholeheartedly endorsed, they are at least perceived as a means of alleviating the pressure of the dilemma of a program's survival versus its integrity.

Level IV decisions. Developmental program goals reflect the language and intent of institutional mission statements and provide a framework for specific program objectives. Administrative processes (the program planning and budgeting cycle, the curriculum committee, for example) are used to articulate the developmental philosophy. Both short-term and long-term goals are negotiated with superiors (New York State Education Department 1977, p. 75). The highest level services possible are implemented within academic areas where goals are compatible.

Variable 6. Attitude toward nontraditional students

In a survey of 38 engineering school programs for the disadvantaged, 80 percent of the faculty stated that the teacher's sensitivity is a "most important" programmatic variable for students' success, exceeded only by students' motivation (97 percent) (Simmons et al. 1979, p. 32).

The traditional predictors of academic success, test scores and high school grades, do not necessarily measure a person's potential to benefit from college (Astin et al. 1972). After one-half century of research, the most sophisticated psychological and statistical methods can account for only 25 percent of the change in achievement indexes (Roueche and Snow 1977, p. 82).

Two conflicting purposes present the developmental planner with a dilemma. The dissemination of information about test scores for individual students is necessary, both to build consensus for developing instruction and to facilitate faculty's advising of individual students. Yet the dissemination of such information to elitist or uninformed faculty members risks prejudicing them against the students who most need expressions of confidence and support. Researchers suggest three methods of resolving this dilemma:

1. Educate the faculty to the limitations of the Scholastic Aptitude Tests. SATs are not aptitude tests and do not measure "capacity for learning," according to Harvard researchers. They are just another standardized achievement test and are a third-rate predictor of success in college, behind high school grades and subject-relevant achievement tests (Slack and Porter 1980).

2. Use criterion-referenced tests instead of standardized survey tests. Criterion-referenced reading tests, constructed from the college textbooks being used, are accurate for identifying specific instructional needs and for demonstrating learning that has occurred (Flippo 1980; Anderson 1973).

Even students of high ability demonstrate surprising specific weaknesses when criterion-referenced tests are used. This use of criterion-referenced tests thus helps to prevent the institutional testing program from embarrassing any one segment of the student population. At one typical college, for example, to be admitted to the nursing program, incoming freshmen must have SAT mathematics scores above 450, which is slightly above the national norm. Yet four consecutive years of testing for fractions, decimals, percents, and ratios (needed to compute dosages) have shown that approximately one-third of the nursing students needed to participate in supplementary instruction (Keimig 1982). The national studies of declining skills corroborate the decline in basic skills among higher ability students as well as others (Carnegie Foundation 1977, pp. 212–13).

3. *Develop local norms for whatever tests are used* (Maxwell 1970). Knowledge about ranking within the institution or the tendency of failure within particular programs to be associated with weaknesses of specific skills is far more useful than national data and norms. Because such information is more situation specific, students are more likely to perceive it as useful rather than demeaning (Roueche and Snow 1977).

The institution's attitude toward students, which tends to become self-fulfilling, is managed by decisions such as these.

Level I decisions. Students face self-defeating disparagement from other students and negative expectations from faculty, which are reinforced by their isolation in remedial programs.

Level II decisions. The student has the problem and can obtain help to overcome it if he or she chooses.

Level III decisions. Within academic courses, appropriate opportunities for review are provided, albeit begrudgingly, because students are needed to populate the programs; to fail to upgrade their skills would damage the program.

Level IV decisions. Students are accepted nonjudgmentally, with positive expectations for success. When perceived as similar to others in the institution, they are more successful (Roueche and Snow 1977). Comprehensive instruction provides for all learning needs without special designations of support components as "remedial."

Variable 7. Structure of the developmental program
The organizational structure of developmental programs has interested researchers since the post-war influx of nontraditional college students (Braken 1954; Bliesmer 1956; Gordon 1975; Arkwardy and Chafin 1980; Sanders 1980). Before that time, the remedial course model was generally assumed, being well suited to the institutional purposes of the time (see McAllister 1954; Causey 1955, 1956, 1957; Robinson 1965 for descriptions of early programs.

The structure of support services has become increasingly complex and varied, with the broadening of institutional purposes for learning improvement programs. Whereas integrated services were rarely reported before the 1950s, in recent decades integrated services have been described more often by program evaluators (Arkwardy and Chafin 1980; Sanders 1980; Fincher 1975, for example).

Research evidence is accumulating to show that integrated services providing an immediate link between the need to know and the learning experience are the most effective (Trillin and Associates 1980; Manzo 1979; Cross 1976). Multilevel, comprehensive services related to regular academic courses allow a degree of individualization that is otherwise unattainable and can meet the most serious learning needs (Ludwig 1977). Academic faculty place high value on the importance of organized support services that use structured formats for tutoring and review (Simmons et al. 1979). Similar surveys exist showing faculty support for isolated remedial programs in institutions where no integrated support services exist (Fairbanks and Snozek 1973). In no instance in this extensive review of the research, however, was a survey found in which faculty, having both alternatives, rejected coordinated, integrated support services in favor of casual assistance or remedial courses. The remedial function of drills in basic skills, however, was considered a highly important component, even in the integrated programs (Simmons et al. 1979).

Each Hierarchy of Decisions highlights the developmental program structure because its significance outweighs all other variables if the developmental program is to fulfill its potential role as catalyst and lead the institution to the reaffirmation of its teaching mission. When the organizational structure of the developmental program fosters involvement of staff in all disciplines and at all levels, programmatic goals, objectives, and rationale evolve to become developmental and hence more effective. Denied this interaction, however, developmental programs tend not to influence the goals, objectives, and rationale that are operationalized in other programs within the college and to have little influence on overall academic achievement and persistence.

The Hierarchy of Decisions Relating to Instructional Methods and Content

Most college learning improvement programs provide learning center services such as tutoring, multimedia materials, diagnosis, and remediation. But most programs differ in the inclusiveness of students likely to be served, whether a targeted high-risk group or all freshmen, for example, and in the comprehen-

Research evidence is accumulating to show that integrated services providing an immediate link between the need to know and the learning experiences are the most effective.

siveness of the goals, objectives, and content of the services provided.

Successful developmental programs are more inclusive and more comprehensive in scope, usually containing several components: reading, grammar, writing, mathematics, science, ethnic studies, study (survival) skills, self-development, and career/life planning (Grant and Hoeber 1978). Programs undertake cognitive development, using the concepts of Perry (Cross 1976, pp. 161–67) and others, as an alternative to accepting low-level thinking as an immutable characteristic in lower achieving students. The inclusion of these various components, however, does not necessarily mean the creation of additional, separate courses.

In Figure 4, the range and ranking of the possible decisions relating to instructional methods and content are charted for the following developmental program variables:

8. methods of instruction
9. responsiveness to students
10. development of cognitive and basic skills
11. affective development of students
12. control for learners' success.

Level III and Level IV decisions are achieved through the systematic link of developmental support services to academic courses. This link expands the course instructor's resources and control of instruction through the creation of a highly flexible delivery system in which a wider range of individual needs can be met. The focus within each variable is on decisions that are made relevant to academic course instruction. The research evidence cited is from studies of programs in which this academic/developmental services link has been made; some of the research reflects academic course faculties' estimation of what has worked for their students.

Variable 8. Methods of instruction

Underprivileged and low-ability students do not always participate in self-paced programs. Other elements are needed as well (Ludwig 1977). Contrary to popular belief, high-ability students achieve better in small discussion classes; low-ability students achieve better in larger classes taught in a benevolently authoritarian manner (Bernstein 1976). Eclectic instruction works best, providing a balanced combination of individualized laboratory practice and class interaction (Wassman 1977).

Asked to indicate the relationship of special teaching methods to students' survival, faculty indicated greater importance for basic skills instruction; teaching concepts; group discussion with tutors, with other students, and with teachers; drill and repetition; and personalized systems of instruction. Faculty also valued video and audiotapes, the inquiry method, the discovery method, interdisciplinary studies, team teaching, and varying teaching styles. No single strategy was positively related to survival by more than 24 percent of the faculty (Simmons et al. 1979, p. 43), which is an indication of the need for a variety of approaches. Engineering faculty reported success for underprepared students with review sessions (50 percent), discussion of homework (48 percent), selection of an understandable text (58 percent), relating discussion to life experiences (29 percent), and tutoring sessions (60 percent) (Simmons et al. 1979, p. 32).

Learning methods should include formal, informal, and incidental learning experiences (Jason et al. 1976; Gordon 1975). Several characteristics of courses are related to students' success: clear goals for students; evaluation through frequent testing; self-paced learning; active, not passive, students; and small modules (Cross 1976).

Level I decisions. Standard methods are used within the academic course. Students experiencing academic difficulty receive no assistance directly with their course work beyond that which benevolent instructors can provide on their own time.

Level II decisions. Standard methods are used within the academic course. Outside tutoring services may provide an alternative, or at least more repetition, for some students.

Level III decisions. Coordinated, supplementary, varied learning experiences are specially designed to augment the usual course presentation for some learning objectives.

Level IV decisions. Eclectic approaches to instruction are used in academic courses, recognizing that no one method will be sufficient for all students and that each method may work best for some. A balanced combination of classroom interpersonal interaction and out-of-class learning assistance provides opportunities for students' participation in class, which is necessary to achieve involvement and cognitive development, and drill/repetition, which are needed to achieve mastery of requisite basic information and skills. The course content is developed sequentially, includes requisite cognitive and basic skills, and is based upon students' diagnosed needs.

Figure 4   The Hierarchy of Decisions

Variables

Possible Decisions

Potential for Improved Learning and Instructional Change

High →

Methods of Instruction	Responsiveness to Students	Development of Cognitive and Basic Skills
Within academic course, use eclectic methods and combination of class interaction and out-of-class drill.	Within academic course, vary teaching time and tasks according to response of students.	Incorporate development of requisite knowledge and skills within ongoing academic curriculum.
Systematically develop other learning experiences for some objectives to augment the course.	Develop selected specific skills in coordinated, supplementary activities.	Develop selected specific skills in coordinated, supplementary activities.
Use standard methods only in academic courses; encourage individuals to seek help from others.	In academic courses, provide same time and tasks for all. Let other services respond to atypical needs.	Assume basic skills and knowledge to be adequate for academic courses.
Use standard methods only in academic courses; provide no individual assistance for academic course work.	Assume that remedial courses will eliminate differences; in academic courses, provide same time and tasks for all.	Teach generic skills in remedial courses; assume those who complete course to be ready for regualar courses.

← Low

Relating to Instructional Methods and Content

Variables

Affective Development of Students	Control for Learners' Success	Structure of Developmental Program
Incorporate personal growth and counseling into academic programs.	Within courses, manage instruction to provide frequent successes; use grades based on competency with absolute learning standards.	IV Comprehensive Learning Systems
Structure series of counseling/advice contacts for all students.	Maintain minimum competency by reteaching and retesting for selected objectives in academic courses.	III Course-related Learning Services
Refer students with emotional problems to counselors for help.	Help individuals become self-directed learners through counseling on their learning problems.	II Individual Learning Assistance
Establish component in applied psychology as a separate course or within an orientation or remedial course.	Allow students to sink or swim in the regular program.	I Remedial Courses

Variable 9. Responsiveness to students

Many educators who seek to meet students' individual learning needs find that it is easier said than done. A survey of community college programs in New Jersey showed that there was little true individualization of students' real needs despite the widespread claims that these programs were individualized (Kahn 1977).

The critical variables for learning are (1) the amount of students' exposure to course material, (2) the amount of time students spend in directed, structured learning situations, and (3) teachers' skills (Maxwell 1979, p. 381). When the task is held constant, the time needed to complete the task varies among students. A sizable amount of evidence supports this view (Grant et al. 1979; Webb 1977).

Teaching methods should be researched and practiced before being used in an academic course. If a particular method is effective with students, it should be retained; if not, it should be discontinued with that particular group (Simmons et al. 1979; Grant and Hoeber 1978). Faculty should vary their teaching style and look for nonverbal responses to lectures (Simmons et al. 1979).

In colleges with successful developmental programs, more faculty feel that the college in general tries to respond to students' needs and desires (68 percent in colleges with successful programs, 48 percent in colleges with unsuccessful programs). Similarly, more students in the colleges with successful developmental programs feel that their colleges generally respond to their needs as students (New York State Education Department 1977, p. 42).

Personalized systems for instruction have been validated for greater effectiveness for long-term learning than the lecture method. Bloom's conclusion was that 95 percent of students can master a subject if sufficient time is allowed. Bloom's basic concept is supported by the research, but not all learners achieve equally (Ludwig 1977). The learning time that can be provided is limited, however, by institutional and personal resources and by students' motivation to persist (Cross 1976).

Tutoring enhances the responsiveness of programs and is effective whether done by course instructors, professional staff, peers, or computers (Cross 1976).

Level I decisions. The assumption is that remedial courses reduce the differences among students and adequately respond to any special needs. Therefore, within academic courses, learning time and tasks are not varied.

Level II decisions. Within academic courses, teaching time and tasks are the same for all. Students who do not respond are encouraged to seek assistance from other sources in the college, such as the developmental program staff or counselors.

Level III decisions. Within academic courses, individual students' needs for some objectives are systematically met through coordinated supplementary activities that provide additional time on a task.

Level IV decisions. Academic faculty use diagnostic information and monitor students' response to instruction, modifying the procedures when necessary. Instructional time and tasks are varied according to individual students' learning needs.

Variable 10. Development of cognitive and basic skills

Many remedial programs seek to improve basic skills in reading and mathematics; however, few concentrate on problem solving. Cognition needs to be taught (Ludwig 1977; Kagan 1973) and abstracting and generalizing skills developed (Whimbey and Lockhead 1981; Simmons et al. 1979).

Low-ability students are oriented toward concrete matters. They have difficulty dealing with abstractions, are inclined to right answers rather than complexities, abstractions, or problem solving, and demonstrate lack of reasoning ability during evaluations. The work of such students may reflect the use of memorized material that cannot be appropriately used in different contexts, confusion when memorized words are used in incorrect multiple choice test items, and interest in answers only, not in processes for obtaining answers (Ludwig 1977).

The extent to which basic scholastic ability can be improved is unknown and subject to question (Kendrick 1969). Students can be taught higher level cognitive processes, at least through the level of application. However, some processes such as analysis, synthesis, and evaluation may be beyond the reach of some learners. Nevertheless, faculty must make an effort to improve students' cognitive functioning in college (Ludwig 1977).

Piaget's research has implications for higher education. Fifty percent of college freshmen are concrete thinkers, the proportion being higher in institutions with open admissions (Killian 1980). Although all people develop reasoning abilities in the same sequence of stages, some adults never achieve formal operations stages, which poses major questions for college planners: How much teaching intervention facilitates the move into formal operations? What constitutes formal operations in the various disciplines, especially history, social studies, and literature? Are the wrong age students in college? The design of instructional programs must include teaching activities for students in various stages (Killian 1980).

Engineering instructors most often correlated the following special teaching methods with effective retention: individualized instruction (45 percent), instruction in basic skills (45 percent), personalized system of instruction (39 percent), and emphasis on concepts (39 percent) (Simmons et al. 1979).

A democratized higher education institution in a pluralistic society must become a multipurpose institution with variable routes to success, with various missions for different students (Gordon 1975).

Level I decisions. Generic reasoning and basic skills are developed in special courses. Students who complete the course are assumed to have achieved "readiness" for regular academic courses and thereafter to have no further need to learn basic skills.

Level II decisions. Students in academic courses are assumed to have achieved mature cognition and mastery of basic skills; therefore, teaching is conducted in the traditional manner. Students may obtain assistance for whatever they may need on their own.

Level III decisions. Certain cognitive and basic skills are developed through coordinated adjunct learning activities.

Level IV decisions. Relevant, requisite basic and cognitive skills are incorporated into the structure of academic courses and programs. (See Killian 1980 and Ludwig 1977 for descriptions of science courses and a history course, respectively, that develop cognition skills.)

Variable 11. Affective development of students

Although researchers increasingly recognize the importance of students' emotional needs in determining their success in college, components and goals for affective development are seldom incorporated into either academic or developmental programs. The primary emphasis on purely cognitive outcomes has resulted in the neglect of such important "informal learnings" as self-concept, locus of control, attitude toward education, and motivation (Renner 1979; Duck 1978; Sherman and Tinto 1975).

Motivation and drive, which are impossible to statistically manipulate or control (McFadden 1979), are nevertheless considered by faculty and researchers to be *the* most important characteristic of students for determining success in college. Motivation and persistence are more important than traditional predictors (such as test scores) of success in college (Renner 1979; Simmons et al. 1979; Donnovan 1977; Lesnick 1972; Meister et al. 1962; Entwisle 1960; Roueche and Kirk 1973).

Poor academic self-image is a cause of failure in college (Grant and Hoeber 1978; Cross 1976). The underprepared student has been victimized by the school and certified an academic failure and is justifiably wary, feeling incompetent and impotent in the educational world (Grant and Hoeber 1978; Glasser 1969). Such students must be helped to overcome fear in a competitive environment (Simmons et al. 1979), a sense of worthlessness, alienation, and hostility (Renner 1979; Jelfo 1974).

Students' genuine involvement in special programs is a necessary precondition for academic success. Three stages of students' involvement—attraction, participation, and sustained involvement—can be used as a barometer to measure the comprehensiveness of developmental programs (Donnovan 1977).

Research results, though tentative, correlate students' locus of control with success in college. Counseling students to become responsible for themselves—to internalize their locus of control—rather than to place responsibility and dependence on schools, parents, and peers is an element in successful programs (Grant and Hoeber 1978). Problem-solving techniques are beneficial for internalizing this locus of control (Ozer 1980; Barshis 1979; Ludwig 1977).

Students' success in college can be predicted from a checklist of behaviors that differentiate successful and unsuccessful students. Success is predicted from such behaviors and attitudes as motivation (committed, ambitious, industrious, responsible), completion of assignments and projects on time, and an orientation toward goals (realistic, flexible, purposeful behavior). Failure in college can be predicted from the persistence of the opposite behaviors and attitudes: a lack of motivation (apathetic, depressed, uncommitted, uninterested); incomplete or late assignments and projects (exhibiting plagiarism, lack of attention to detail, repeated errors, an inability to generalize concepts); and a lack of orientation toward goals (erratic, irresponsible, nonpurposeful behavior) (New York State Education Department 1977, Appendix C).

Students' success in college can be predicted from a check list of behaviors that differentiate successful and unsucessful students.

Counseling assists "personhood development" (Jelfo 1974) and helps the student make realistic choices, establish career goals (which are related to persistence in college), assert inner control, and become more purposeful in daily behaviors in the academic life. Both peer and professional counseling are effective (Cross 1976).

Level I decisions. A component in applied personal psychology to enhance students' affective development is incorporated within a basic skills course or an orientation course or is established as a separate course.

Level II decisions. Students with emotional problems are referred to counselors for help.

Level III decisions. A series of counseling/advising contacts is established to systematically achieve certain specific affective objectives for all students in the academic program.

Level IV decisions. Affective goals are incorporated in the design of instructional programs. Facilitative experiences are provided for the development of self-concept and problem-solving abilities to foster internal locus of control (Brawer 1982). Counseling and advising to enhance positive behaviors, to help students develop career goals, and to improve overall motivation are ongoing activities within academic programs.

Variable 12. Control for learners' success

Teachers and managers must provide opportunities for success and rewards for students while simultaneously providing challenging experiences (Simmons et al. 1979). The mastery of skills enhances students' self-concept, sense of personal worth, internal control, and the creation of positive expectations (Grant and Hoeber 1978). Successful encounters with learning raise expectations; repeated failures lower them. Successful learning experiences strengthen self-motivated persistence and overcome passivity (Arkwardy and Chafin 1980; Cross 1976; Bruner 1973).

Management and control for success are achieved through the use of diagnostic instruction, grades based on competence, responsibility for learning, and organization of the course content.

Assessing requisite skills for freshmen courses and entering students' abilities provides a "contrast profile" of particular skills to be developed for each student (Roueche and Snow 1977, p. 83). This assessment is used to guide planning and instruction for academic programs and for remedial programs.

Effective education is the product of a match between learners' characteristics, the learning environment, and learning tasks (Gordon 1975).

Grading should be based on competency, with an absolute grading standard to reflect mastery (Grant and Hoeber 1978; Donnovan 1977; Cross 1976). Reteaching and repeating tests up to three times improve learning; the fourth time does not (Donnovan 1977).

Under such conditions, achievement in a course depends less on students' entering skills or abilities. Correlation between aptitude and achievement is typically lower under mastery learning than under other instructional programs. The slowest students have the time they need, and the systematic structure allows for necessary remedial assistance in a regular, prescribed manner. Learning outcomes rather than teacher behaviors are emphasized (Ludwig 1977).

In the past, compensatory education has tended to shift the responsibility for learning more to the teacher than to the student (Gordon 1975). Students must, can, and should, however, assume more responsibility for their own learning (Cross 1979). The design of instructional material featuring mastery learning and individualized methods causes students to assume responsibility for achieving goals in a flexible schedule; teachers and students plan together to overcome a particular difficulty and retest when necessary (Renner 1979).

Within the course, clear statements of objectives enable students to know the outcomes required; courses should also provide different formats and alternate routes for reaching those objectives (Cross 1979). Communicating positive expectations for success and sequencing instruction from the more easily understood concepts to the more complex ones are associated with successful programs (Simmons et al. 1979 Roueche and Snow 1977).

Level I decisions. Students are allowed to sink or swim as best they can in the regular academic program. Remedial courses attempt to teach students how to learn.

Level II decisions. The rescue of some students is attempted through tutoring services. Students are helped to become more self-directed, effective learners through the use of problem-solving techniques applied to the course in which they are experiencing difficulty (Maxwell 1975).

Level III decisions. Minimum competency on some course objectives is maintained through the use of adjunct learning experiences and retesting.

Level IV decisions. Instruction within the academic course is managed so as to provide frequent successful learning encounters for all students. Grades based on competency to an absolute standard and retesting when necessary are used instead of relative or curved grading standards. Clearly communicated objectives and alternative routes for learning ensure an opportunity for success for most students.

Learning improvement and program structure

The most effective instructional system for learning would not be thought of as a learning improvement program, because most of the services provided by the developmental personnel would be fully incorporated into academic courses. It is very difficult, however, to change, through formal administrative procedures, the way academic instruction is organized and delivered.

For this reason, the structure of the developmental program within the college determines, more than any other single variable, the ability of the program to influence academic instruction and thereby genuinely improve learning. If resources for the developmental program are expended in a structure of activities that directly supports academic courses, then course instructors' capabilities are greatly expanded and eclectic, diagnostic instructional methods in academic courses are possible. Atypical and extreme needs can be responded to, and relevant cognitive and basic skills and affective development can be provided. Furthermore, academic faculty and curriculum leaders perceive as helpful the evolving reorganizations of instruction that they themselves have helped design.

This process works both ways. Integrated services lead to a changing organizational structure for the developmental program as well, changes that are well received by the faculty whose classroom problems are being ameliorated but may be hardly noticed by anyone else.

The Hierarchy of Decisions Relating to Institutional Policies and Standards

Ultimately, to become permanent, these changes in structure must be established in the policies of departments, divisions, and the college or university. One manifestation of administrative support for an improvement in learning is the academic policies and standards that are established and enforced within the institution (Arkwardy and Chafin 1980). Standards imply achievement of genuine learning, which is more than "merely succeeding" (McCabe 1981). Figure 5 indicates the range of possible decisions for each of the following variables relating to institutional policies and standards:

13. directing students into appropriate courses and programs
14. definition of competencies in academic courses
15. credit earned for remedial developmental study
16. systematic procedures for advisement
17. organization of the developmental program within the college
18. institutionalization of developmental services.

Variable 13. Directing students into appropriate courses and programs

It is rare to find a college that has not modified its admissions standards in the last 10 years (Grant and Hoeber 1978). Colleges are coping with kinds of students not previously educated to this level. Current controversies are similar to the debate about secondary schools in the 1890s and 1900s, the central issue today being the adequacy of the higher education system to absorb and adapt to its new clientele (Grant et al. 1979, p. 8). The average high school graduate today has a "B" average over four years of high school yet reads at the eighth grade level, a loss of two grade levels in the last 10 years (Roueche 1981–82, p. 17).

Controversy has raged over whether underprepared students should be required to participate in remedial courses. Some studies show a decline during the 1970s in the number of institutions mandating remedial courses, perhaps indicating the trend of the future (Grant and Hoeber 1978). Of institutions surveyed in 1977, 89 percent did not require the courses (p. 28). The New York State Education Department study (1977) also favors voluntary enrollment in remedial courses, which students would accept when counseled properly.

Three studies over a four-year period involving large numbers of students at the Bronx Community College show a different outcome, however. Although many students did enroll, high percentages of students, ranging from 14 to 65 percent,

Figure 5 The Hierarchy of Decisions:
Variables

	Directing Students	Definition of Competencies	Credit Earned for Developmental Study
	Use placement tests and achievement indicators as the bases for academic program planning.	In academic courses, specify minimum competencies for entry and exit	Award credit for remedial/ developmental study whether in skills courses or as part of the assigned work in an academic course.
	Pretest for some objectives; use results for some requirements and assignments.	In academic courses, specify minimum competency for selected objectives.	
	Allow students to elect or reject individual diagnosis, advice, and remediation.	Assume availability of assistance to ensure adequate learning.	Disallow credit for participation in skills courses or supplementary remedial work.
	Allow students' participation in remediation to be voluntary.	Adjust learning standard by curving grades in academic courses.	

Possible Decisions
Potential for Improved Learning and Instructional Change

High

Low

Relating to Institutional Policies and Standards

Variables

Advisement Procedures for Systematic	Organization of Developmental Program within College	Degree of Institutional- ization	Structure of Developmental Program
Monitor students' progress. Enforce policies for quality and direction of students. Use diagnostic information in program planning.	Establish division to lead, staff, and coordinate skills courses presented in other academic divisions.	Integrate developmental concept into college policies, problem solving, and curricula through participation of developmental staff on committees.	IV Comprehensive Learning Systems
	Establish division to coordinate support services and present its own courses.	Integrate developmental concept into policy requirements of congenial, cooperating departments and courses.	III Course-related Learning Services
Advise students routinely through typical course sequences. Use advisors who lack information about students' basic skills achievement, personal goals, and learning needs.	Subordinate leadership of developmental services within another division or precollege unit.	Establish developmental concept in individual services to students and faculty.	II Individual Learning Assistance
	Scatter skills courses among existing divisions with no autonomy and little or no coordination.	Seek interdisciplinary links and contacts to overcome isolation of skills courses.	I Remedial Courses

chose to bypass the courses (Bronx Community College 1974, 1975; Eagle 1977).

The impact of large numbers of underprepared students on the practices and standards within regular courses has rarely been considered in research studies. It has been assumed that traditional academic standards would prevail and that instructors would fail inept students who chose to bypass courses teaching basic skills and enter regular programs. What has occurred instead is a drift of standards so great that it has threatened the credibility of all of higher education and particularly of community college general education programs, where free access despite academic deficiencies has been provided, even to "semiliterate" and "illiterate" students (Cohen 1979). Students from community colleges have a higher attrition rate than other students after they transfer to four-year institutions (Roueche 1981–82). Cohen (1979) associates the increased interest in junior year examinations to four-year colleges' efforts to deal with the extremes of ability among junior-year transfer students.

Mandatory placement in skills courses is associated with successful programs (Roueche and Snow 1977). Current opinion links participation in developmental services with the maintenance of standards in the overall academic program (Roueche 1981–82; Arkwardy and Chafin 1980), a connection that heretofore has been largely ignored.

Robert H. McCabe, President of Miami-Dade Community College, initiated major changes in policy to upgrade the standards of achievement of students at his institution, among them the controlled flow of deficient students through remedial programs and restricted schedules until students demonstrate their ability to perform successfully. Given these controls, faculty will be able to provide instruction to students "within a narrower range of academic competence," thus increasing the likelihood of success (McCabe 1981, p. 10). Only if a student body is properly prepared in basic skills can standards be maintained in other courses (Trillin and Associates 1980, p. 262).

Restricting high-risk students' first-semester credit hours and guiding their selection of courses to those in which they have a chance of succeeding have been verified as ways to enhance long-term success (Barshis 1979). If students' skills are adequate, their participation in a support program alone might be justified. If they are inadequate, remediation is a must (Simmons et al. 1979). Working students must not be permitted to enroll for a full academic course load (Roueche 1981–82). Students with deficiencies who begin programs should be expected to take longer to finish them (Roueche 1981–82; McCabe 1981).

Placement testing of all students who enter the college is necessary to enable the college to provide proper direction to its students. Colleges should develop their own local norms and determine their own success thresholds for whatever tests are used (Roueche 1981–82; New York State Education Department 1977; Cross 1976).

Level I decisions. Participation in remediation is voluntary. Learning specialists' recommendations are not communicated to advisors and not used in students' academic planning.

Level II decisions. Students may elect or reject individual diagnosis, advisement, and remediation. Learning specialists' recommendations about which courses to select may or may not be used in students' academic planning.

Level III decisions. Within an academic course, pretesting for some objectives provides a basis for some required supplementary assignments.

Level IV decisions. For all incoming students, placement testing provides the basis for directing students into appropriate courses, supplementary study, and schedules. Credit hours for high-risk and working students are restricted until students demonstrate their ability to do more.

Variable 14. Definition of competencies in academic courses
No absolute standards of competency exist for college courses and degrees. Standards for entry and exit must be defined for courses and programs (Cohen 1979; Jelfo 1974). It is patronizing to students to modify standards; to do so implies that they are incapable (Gordon 1975). "Colleges must make a commitment to standards . . . " (McCabe 1981, p. 10).

Considerable national interest exists for defining the competencies to be obtained from a college education. Government officials and state accreditation agencies increasingly seek accountability as a condition of funding (*Chronicle* 16 December 1981; Magarrell 1980; Fincher 1975). Colleges must establish and enforce high performance standards for credit and degrees (Arkwardy and Chafin 1980); otherwise, society will reject the institutions. There must be a point at which it is determined that a student is not going to succeed in the institution and that further investment is not justified (McCabe 1981).

Considerable national interest exists for defining the competencies to be obtained from a college education.

The College Outcome Measures Project (COMP) is a cooperative effort of approximately 130 participating colleges and the American College Testing program (ACT) to define and measure the competencies obtained from general education in college. Several "generations" of tests have been used and a data base accumulated, through which institutions can assess the relative effectiveness of their programs (ACT Program 1980).

Level I decisions. In academic courses, standards are adjusted by curving grades and/or changing requirements. The acceptable level of competency is allowed to fluctuate with the norm of each group of students taking the course.

Level II decisions. The availability of tutorial assistance to individuals is assumed to ensure adequate learning by weaker students.

Level III decisions. In academic courses, minimum competency for some objectives is specified and required of all students.

Level IV decisions. In academic courses, minimum acceptable competencies for most objectives are specified. Prerequisite entry-level skills are published to guide the placement of students and any concurrent (or preenrollment) remediation indicated.

Variable 15. Credit earned for remedial/developmental study

Should credit for graduation be earned in remedial/developmental courses and supplementary study? This issue has been a divisive one, although the trend is to award credit. In a 1977 survey, 65 percent of responding institutions indicated that they grant credit for such courses (Grant and Hoeber 1978). Institutions should give credit (Cross 1976; Jelfo 1974), especially if courses are required (Grant and Hoeber 1978). The granting of credit is associated with successful learning improvement programs (Roueche and Snow 1977) and is necessary to motivate students to take the courses seriously.

Low-potential decisions. Credit is not awarded for remedial/developmental study.

High-potential decisions. Remedial/developmental study earns credit, either as an individual course or as part of the assigned work for grades within an academic course.

Variable 16. Systematic procedures for advisement

Traditional advisement and counseling services are inadequate to help students understand their options, registration policies, program requirements, and other components of the educational system. In addition, a strategy of academic intervention is needed, which will incorporate student orientation and provide systematic monitoring of students' progress and regular follow-up (Boylan 1980).

Implementing policies that allow performance, not time in the program, to determine a student's rate of progress and enforcing performance standards will increase the time needed by many students to complete their programs. Typical descriptions of program sequences and time frames are inappropriate and should be eliminated (Roueche 1981–82). Students will pursue unique combinations of courses and complete requirements at individual, atypical times.

Advising students, traditionally routine and perfunctory, must become personalized. Diagnostic information about students' abilities and complex information about course and program requirements must be interpreted for students and used to help them choose appropriate courses in which they can realistically be expected to succeed. Information about students' progress must be given to advisors, and a system of monitoring progress toward the completion of program goals must be established.

Low-potential decisions. Students are routinely advised through typical course sequences by faculty advisors who lack diagnostic information about students' individual instructional needs.

High-potential decisions. Systematic procedures for monitoring students' progress, initiating intervention, and enforcing policy and standards are implemented. An information system to support the use of diagnostic information in the selection of courses and the planning of the program is established.

Variable 17. Organization of the developmental program within the college

Two categories of problems are associated with the administration of learning improvement programs: (1) those that concern the integration of the services into the existing structures of the college and (2) those that concern the leadership and administration of the program itself (Kingston 1955). The literature reviewed for this monograph supports the integration of developmental instruction into the academic programs of the college and recommends many ways to better integrate services.

Establishing remedial courses in already existing departments is easier in terms of administration, but the evidence suggests that establishing a separate department or division of developmental studies is more effective (Grant and Hoeber 1978; Jelfo 1974). A division or department is characterized by its own administrative leader, who plans, coordinates, and allocates funds. This structure has several advantages: the ability of the division to conduct systematic, collegewide assessments of needs, to develop and promote the program, and to be a highly visible center for innovation and change (Roueche and Snow 1977). The most successful programs have their own space, which is centrally located on campus (Donnovan 1977). They have their own staff and have easy access. Students perceive locations that are difficult to reach as demeaning (New York State Education Department 1977).

Developmental programs organized around a department or division accounted for 67 percent of the successful college programs in one study. Programs consisting of fragmented courses scattered throughout other divisions tended to be less successful, as did programs comprised of regular faculty attached to their own departments who worked with counselors (Roueche and Snow 1977, pp. 89–90).

Successfully integrated programs use a variety of unique and flexible arrangements in which developmental faculty working with regular faculty coordinate objectives for basic and regular instruction (see Roueche and Snow 1977, sec. 3). Courses in basic skills are most successful when they are perceived as regular courses within an academic department's academic program —courses that some students are placed in as a result of testing and that others exempt. No commitments to award credit for exemption are necessary or implied by exemption.

The staff of developmental programs should have a "larger" role in the college's academic decision making to avoid feelings of alienation and to bring their insight and influence to bear in planning. Developmental faculty should be appointed to administrative positions and to faculty committees, which would have the additional benefits of improving students' and faculty's perception of them as "real" teachers (Simmons et al. 1979). It would improve the perception of the program as having a central, vital role, not an ancillary one (New York State Education Department 1977).

Level I decisions. Courses in basic skills are scattered among existing divisions with little or no coordination.

Level II decisions. The leadership of the developmental program is subordinated within another division or precollege unit.

Level III decisions. A developmental division coordinates support services and presents its own courses.

Level IV decisions. A developmental division administers the program through a leader who plans, coordinates, and allocates funds for a comprehensive program. Developmental faculty participate in college and academic decision making. Developmental courses and components are subsumed into the regular course sequences within the academic divisions but are staffed and coordinated by the developmental division.

Variable 18. Institutionalization of developmental services

Decisions about policies and standards reflect the extent to which a college has institutionalized the developmental concept and developmental services into its academic mainstream. The four levels of decisions within the Hierarchies represent these varying degrees of institutional commitment. They comprise as well the sequence of stages through which developmental leaders gain influence and help to shape decisions about policies and standards within the college.

Level I decisions. Interdisciplinary links, contacts, and opportunities for service are sought to enlarge the influence of the developmental program beyond the constraints of isolated courses in basic skills.

Level II decisions. The developmental concept is established in individual, voluntary service to students and teachers.

Level III decisions. The developmental concept is written into policy, requirements, and procedures of congenial departments and courses. Consensus for the concept of a developmental program is evolving; however, an agenda for the developmental program for the curriculum or institution is not yet recognized.

Level IV decisions. The chair of the developmental program and the developmental faculty serve on college committees and strive to integrate the developmental concept into policy statements, design of curricula, and problem-solving processes. Statements describing requirements for proficiency and procedures for reinforcement and remediation are specified for appropriate courses, levels, and transitions in the college. These statements are published in catalogs and syllabi.

The relationship between the enforcement of policies and standards and the structure of learning services

The enforcement of policies that guide students into and through appropriate academic programs and maintain prescribed performance standards can be expected to improve students' achievement. However, merely declaring policy statements that are not carried out is of little value. The structure of the learning services within the institution determines the extent to which such policies are enforceable, given the practical constraints of the contemporary higher education environment.

Level IV, comprehensive, multiservice programs provide the flexibility of courses in basic skills and alternative instructional arrangements through which resources can be efficiently applied for students' specific needs. Such flexibility is important for gaining students' acceptance of performance standards and for providing for individual problems that otherwise would result in waivers of requirements.

For example, a frequent problem in four-year colleges is the transfer student who needs remediation of a basic skill despite having transferred with acceptable credit for related general education courses. Consortium agreements with other colleges or other practical considerations may preclude the requirement of an in-house version of a course for which another college has awarded credit. However, the remediation can be accomplished through mandated competency requirements and individual learning assistance or course-related instructional requirements. Given the fact that one-third of all college students are transfer students (Cohen 1979), feasible, enforceable ways to ensure that transfer students have basic skills are significant considerations in the design of developmental programs.

The Hierarchy of Decisions Relating to Professional and Paraprofessional Staff and Roles

The changing environment for teaching and the increasing diversity of students place demands on teachers for new kinds of skills. Figure 6 shows the ranking of the possible decisions relating to professional and paraprofessional staff and roles for the following variables:

19. regular course instructor's role
20. developmental program staff and role
21. counseling staff and role
22. faculty and staff development.

The variables are ranked according to whether they have high or low potential for improving students' learning and effecting instructional development.

Variable 19. Regular course instructor's role

The academic instructor is the content specialist and the manager of the instructional process (Arkwardy and Chafin 1980). In the Loop College Individual Needs Program, a program identified as highly successful for developing students' achievement (Roueche 1981–82), the course instructor is a "focusing agent" for the student and is learner-centered and caring (Barshis 1979).

Teaching faculty can manipulate six closely related aspects of the learning environment to fit students' learning styles and needs: (1) content—the subject matter, sequence, and pace; (2) classroom format and structure—the mix among alternative teaching strategies; (3) noninstructor-centered, out-of-class activities—homework, fieldwork, supplementary activities; (4) instructor-centered, out-of-class activities and meetings with individuals and groups; (5) evaluation modes; (6) personal style and classroom climate—style of interaction between instructor and student and among students (warmth versus coolness, personal visibility and role modeling versus low-key profile) (Bess 1979, p. 260).

In one study, engineering faculty stated that as teachers they need to understand that the purpose of a teacher is to serve as a mediator between content and student, that they may sometimes need to move outside their classrooms into other experimental learning situations such as seminars and informal occasions, that students are "overwhelmingly" dissatisfied with teaching and the quality of instruction, and that interdisciplinary approaches are superior for some purposes (Simmons et al. 1979).

Low-potential decisions. Academic course instructors function primarily as "passive purveyors of information" (Arkwardy and Chafin 1980, p. 113).

High-potential decisions. Academic course instructors focus on learners' needs and responses, manipulate the learning environment to improve learners' achievement of course objectives, and use developmental program resources to extend the range of options and support available to their students.

Figure 6 The Hierarchy of Decisions: Relating to Variables

	Course Instructor's Role	Developmental Staff and Role
High	Manage learner-centered instructional process. Interact with developmental program staff to extend range of options for learning.	Use a multilevel staff. Make a specialist available to consult and collaborate with academic faculty.
Low	Teach course content, information in traditional, inflexible ways. Provide few alternative learning activities.	Use professional staff only. Restrict specialists primarily to remedial teaching.

Possible Decisions
Potential for Improved Learning and Instructional Change

Professional and Paraprofessional Staff and Roles

Variables

Counseling Staff and Role	Faculty and Staff Development	Structure of Developmental Program
Coordinate counselor-student contact within academic programs. For academic faculty, develop skills as advisors and counselors.	Use informal and formal settings for instructional problem solving as a staff development activity. Regular faculty and developmental specialists collaborate to develop needed techniques.	IV Comprehensive Learning Systems III Course-related Learning Services
Isolate counseling and advising within separate facilities.	Ignore staff development needs.	II Individual Learning Assistance I Remedial Courses

Variable 20. Developmental program staff and role

The developmental program uses a multilevel staff, including professionals, paraprofessionals, and volunteers.

The influence of the learning specialist is increasing. Formerly ignored in academic decisions about students, learning specialists are increasingly asked for assistance by academic faculty attempting to meet the needs of underprepared students (Maxwell 1979, p. 386; Pinette and Smith 1979; Walter 1979). They are increasingly asked to provide specific services such as conducting workshops for faculty and students and developing modules on vocabulary, comprehension, and other topics (Adams 1974).

Successful programs use well-trained peer helpers and other paraprofessionals such as graduate assistants and teaching assistants (Awkwardy and Chafin 1980; Simmons et al. 1979; Maxwell 1979; Wassman 1977; New York State Education Department 1977; Roueche and Snow 1977; Gordon 1975; Jelfo 1974). The use of such affordable helpers as tutors, counselors, and clerical aides enlarges the developmental program's capability to enhance resources for academic courses as well as its own courses. Peer helpers are particularly successful with students.

Low-potential decisions. Restrict the learning specialist's role to teaching remedial courses and use professional staff only.

High-potential decisions. Use a multilevel staff. Make a learning specialist available to consult and collaborate with academic faculty.

Variable 21. Counseling staff and role

Counselors must get out of their offices (Roueche and Snow 1977, p. 122). Faculty must develop special sensitivity to their students. Faculty, in both formal and informal advising situations, must have the skills to communicate positively instructional needs and options. They must respond appropriately to resilient learners, who have the energy to learn; to reluctant learners, who are affected by past histories of failure; and to naive learners, who mistakenly believe as a result of being rewarded for nonachievement that they have certain skills (Arkwardy and Chafin 1980). Cognitive gains may be much less important in the long run the changes in attitude, which are infinitely harder to bring about (Grant and Hoeber 1978).

Low-potential decisions. Counseling contacts are available to students only within a separate facility.

High-potential decisions. Academic faculty develop sensitivity and skills as advisors/counselors to students and incorporate counseling in their programs for their students' affective development.

Variable 22. Faculty and staff development
The average faculty member must learn new methods to deal with the range of abilities confronted in the classroom (Cross 1979). Sixty-three percent of engineering faculty considered themselves inadequate to teach underprepared students and mentioned their needs for training in evaluation, diagnosis, traditional and new methods of teaching, development of curriculum, and organizational development, including team building, decision making, and problem solving (Simmons et al. 1979, p. 17).

Faculty and staff must be energetically involved in both planning and implementing for staff development to have lasting effect (Simmons et al. 1979; New York State Education Department 1977). In a time of steady and declining enrollments with concomitant diminishing resources, it is important to reorient the educational system to create self-directed learners (Cross 1979).

Low-potential decisions. Staff development is not undertaken in formal or informal contacts.

High-potential decisions. Developmental and academic faculty collaborate for staff development that focuses on instructional problem solving and development.

The relationship between professional roles and the structure of the learning improvement program
Ongoing, mutual staff development occurs as a natural consequence of the collaboration of developmental and academic faculty to develop learning activities for students. Resistance to change is diminished when faculty seek assistance to solve students' learning problems in their programs. The structure of a developmental program is thus the most important variable for achieving effective staff development. Developmental program models that foster interdisciplinary contact facilitate staff development. Program models that isolate learning specialists inhibit the ongoing, problem-solving contacts through which academic faculty might be influenced to use new methods and acquire new skills.

Faculty and staff must be energetically involved in both planning and implementing for staff development to have a lasting effect.

The Hierarchy of Decisions Relating to the
Evaluation of Learning Improvement Programs

What should be measured, and how, in the evaluation of learning improvement programs when the values being sought are improved GPA and retention? Evaluation is the " . . . process of delineating, obtaining, and providing useful information for judging decision alternatives . . . " (Stufflebeam 1971, p. 37). Because students' learning outcomes and the impact of the remedial/developmental program are enhanced or constrained by the decisions of many people within the college, the scope of the evaluation must be such that all decision makers have accurate information about the effects of all the controllable variables that are relevant to a particular instructional setting—including students' behavior, developmental and regular program practices, and institutional policies.

The Hierarchies in the aggregate contain a comprehensive list of variables that research has demonstrated to be significant in the design of learning improvement programs. Determining the institutional status of each of these variables provides a framework for evaluation and the subsequent improvement of remedial/developmental and academic programs.

Figure 7 ranks the possible decisions relating to the evaluation of learning improvement programs for four critical variables:

23. institutional context and outcomes
24. student outcomes
25. academic standards and the grade point average
26. ongoing evaluation.

Variable 23. Institutional context and outcomes

The more successful remedial/developmental programs are characterized by a high degree of integration of developmental services, philosophy, and staff within the academic life of the institution. So it is with evaluation itself. All aspects of policy, regular programs, and institutional context that affect the developmental program, influence the learning of students, and/or establish the standards by which students are judged must be considered if the study is to account for a significant proportion of the factors affecting students' learning (Roueche and Snow 1977, p. 104; Gordon 1975).

Success in effective programs is measured against the institution's long-term goals and its short-term performance objectives (New York State Education Department 1977, p. 74) and exter-

nal standards of accountability when they are applicable (Mc-
Fadden 1979). The criteria of success may be better
performance in the next level class as well as better test scores
(Maxwell 1970, 1979; Cross 1976). Local definitions of success are legitimate. For example, in light of extraordinary circumstances of background, a modest rate of persistence of 40
percent might show success (Donnovan 1977).

In strong programs, institutional outcomes are assessed in addition to student outcomes; those institutional outcomes might
include the most efficacious allocation of resources, revisions
of admissions criteria and program standards, greater program
visibility and acceptance, staff development, increased cooperation and communication among faculty, and a broader base of
support (New York State Education Department 1977). Although it is important to understand the impact of programs for
the disadvantaged on their institutions, almost nothing is known
about the subject (Richardson et al. 1981; Donnovan 1977).
Evidence of institutional response and change toward more use
of developmental concepts is sought.

Several levels within the college are involved in the evaluation, including the developmental program staff, the academic
program staff, and participating program administrators (Simmons et al. 1979; New York State Education Department
1977). Evaluators should ask several questions: What is the relation of the developmental program evaluation to the regular
academic program evaluation? Are the appropriate academic
faculty involved in diagnosis and setting standards for the
learning services and skills courses? Does scheduling allow
interaction and cooperation with other faculty? Do opportunities
exist for staffing dual assignments? (New York State Education
Department 1977).

Level I decisions. Although overall learning, represented by
data on GPA and persistence, may be used as a criterion of
success, the outcomes are explained only in terms of the remedial program. The influence of the college's policies and academic program practices is not examined.

Level II decisions. Some institutional factors are considered
in evaluating the assistance given to individual students; however, the college's practices are not systematically described,
evaluated, or recommended for their effect on learning.

Level III decisions. Instruction and other relevant factors
within an associated academic course or program are included

Figure 7 The Hierarchy of Decisions: Relating to Variables

	Institutional Context and Outcomes	Student Outcomes
High ↑	Analyze all relevant regular faculty practices, institutional factors, circumstances, and outcomes; make institutional recommendations.	Assess changes based on criterion tasks related to the content of services and course, on grades, and on indices in academic courses.
	Analyze selected relevant features within an adjunct academic course.	Within an academic course, assess change using criterion tasks for a few integrated developmental activities as in Level IV.
	Mention some institutional factors pertaining to assisted students. Do not systematically analyze institutional factors.	Assess changes using general tests and academic course grades.
Low ↓	Exclude institutional factors, effects, academic faculty. Study students and remedial program only.	Assess outcomes with no analysis of change.

Possible Decisions
Potential for Improved Learning and Instructional Change

the Evaluation of Learning Improvement Programs

Variables

Academic Standards and GPA	Ongoing Evaluation	Structure of Developmental Program
Analyze competencies represented by GPA. Assess relationship between developmental and regular programs.	Assess and provide perfodic feedback. Use follow-up studies. Analyze long-term effects, changes.	IV Comprehensive Learning Systems
Within adjunct or follow-on course, assess relationship between regular and remedial instruction and competencies represented by grade criteria.	Monitor changes through a course and a follow-on course.	III Course-related Learning Services
Use grades in verbal or quantitative courses as a criterion of the effectiveness of assistance to individuals.	Limit evaluation to a single semester.	II Individual Learning Assistance
Use GPA as a criterion for discrete skills courses. Assume relevance of skills and course work to the content represented by GPA.	Undertake no systematic evaluation of the developmental program on overall, long-term learning.	I Remedial Courses

in the evaluation of developmental services. The regular course instructor participates in the evaluation.

Level IV decisions. Regular faculty as well as developmental faculty are involved in planning and implementing the evaluation. The evaluation of the learning improvement program is perceived in relation to the college's mission and to its overall instructional program. Using a variety of indices, it assesses regular program and institutional status, needs, and change. It produces recommendations for institutional policy and changes in the regular program as well as in the developmental program.

Variable 24. Student outcomes

Academic performance is the ultimate validator of a learning improvement program. Appropriate measures include survival in the regular program and completion of the degree (Simmons et al. 1979; Gordon 1975) and such indices as GPA and grades in certain subsequent courses (Boylan 1981; Roueche and Snow 1977; Sparks and Davis 1977; Cross 1976; Maxwell 1970).

The value-added concept is increasingly important in times of scarce resources. Therefore, researchers seek evidence of change and improvement. Student outcomes are judged relative to students' entry level aptitudes (Arkwardy and Chafin 1980; McFadden 1979; Baird 1977; Roueche and Snow 1977).

The measurement of change for remedial students is difficult because of the statistical and research design problems discussed previously. The success of developmental programs depends in part on the criteria used (Cross 1976); many indices are preferable to a few (Barrow 1980; Trillin and Associates 1980; Roueche and Snow 1977). Success must be defined in relation to both institutional and individual goals. For example, a failure to persist in a particular college might not represent a failure in cases where students are helped to clarify their own goals and to find employment or to transfer to another school (New York State Education Department 1977; Roueche and Snow 1977).

Standardized tests do not measure the specific reading skills that are developed in particular courses (Maxwell 1979; Anderson 1973) and thus tend to understate the growth that may have occurred in reading ability (Flippo 1980). Results are likely to be more accurate and favorable when such variables are measured as the attainment of a specific skill, the application of skills and knowledge in regular program courses, retention, the rates of continuation and success (as defined locally), academic status, attitudes and behaviors such as attendance and class participation, commitment, and decision-making skills (Walvekar 1981, pp. 75–94; New York State Education Department 1977, p. 741). Criterion measures consistent with the objectives of the program are preferable to standardized tests, which are inappropriate for measuring an individual student's growth (Arkwardy and Chafin 1980; Anderson 1973; Maxwell 1979, p. 221). A student's performance of the criterion task should be interpreted in relation to the specific performance standards, should reflect the instructional intent, and should generalize to the domain of instructionally relevant tasks in subsequent courses (Arkwardy and Chafin 1980).

More accurate measures of academic success may be the key to making basic educational processes more meaningful in developmental programs. Interest is emerging in measuring learning processes as well as level of achievement; however, few useful instruments exist for doing so (Gordon 1975). Acceptable evidence includes data about interactions, small group feedback, indicators of attitude, and procedural research (New York State Education Department 1977; Gordon 1975). The "acceptability" of evidence is established by its appropriateness for the purpose for which it is used (Moore 1981; Maxwell 1979).

The grouping statistic, whether a cut-off score or an average, will affect the result obtained from evaluation (Trillin and Associates 1980). When a mean is the measure, it is a statistical fact that by definition half the people will always be below average (Cross 1976, pp. 9–13). If a remedial program is limited to the weakest students, assistance to them may result in a "C" performance in a follow-on course for which the average grade is "B." Comparing these scores could discredit the remedial program and mask genuine gains in learning (Maxwell 1979). Criterion-referenced cut-off scores are therefore more meaningful indicators of success than are average scores.

Level I decisions. Student outcomes are assessed without an analysis of their entry-level abilities.

Level II decisions. Student growth is assessed using general criteria for tests and grades.

Level III decisions. Within an academic course, students' learning and change are assessed for each of those objectives for which developmental and regular instructional activities have been integrated. Specific skills and knowledge are measured by means of criterion tasks that are related to support of the developmental program and to content of the regular academic program. Grades in the regular program are a measure of success in the developmental program.

Level IV decisions. Within academic courses, students' learning and change are assessed using many indices of participation, persistence, and commitment. The same criterion tasks and criteria of success for Level III decisions are used.

Variable 25. Academic standards and the grade point average
Why does GPA as a criterion of success provide such inconsistent results as reported in the many studies in which it has been used? Do these findings reflect the inefficacy of the programs being evaluated or the inadequacy of GPA as a criterion? What is the proper use of GPA as a criterion in learning improvement programs?

Of itself, GPA is not a consistent standard, either among programs within a school or among colleges. Grading practices vary among faculty, departments, and colleges; grading standards vary with changes in admissions policy or skills of admitted students (Gordon 1975). Because remedial programs work with the least prepared students, the apparent result of the program can be influenced by drifts in the admitted students' ability profiles (Maxwell 1979, p. 189).

Research does not support the use of GPA as the only criterion, but it does support it as one of the possible bases for judgment (Tillman 1973; Maxwell 1979). Furthermore, grade-related criteria such as GPA, success in follow-on courses, and the relation of credit hours earned to credit hours attempted are appropriate measures only when the developmental program is designed to supplement the regular curriculum, not when it operates as a discrete program (Webb 1977).

A definition of the standards of competence required in the courses that contribute to GPA and the relevance of those standards to the content of the developmental program must be demonstrated for GPA to be a meaningful criterion. This information is not provided in many studies in which GPA is used as a criterion, however, particularly studies of isolated remedial reading programs. The omission of this information may account for the inconsistency of the results obtained in these studies.

In effective programs, the evaluations have provided answers to several questions about how developmental studies interface with the regular academic program: (1) Are valid entrance and exit standards established? (2) Are regular faculty aware of the standards? (3) Is the diagnosis of students' needs specific enough to guide instruction? (New York State Education Department 1977).

Level I decisions. GPA is used as a criterion of the effectiveness of remedial skills courses, which are assumed to be generally relevant to the content of the academic program.

Level II decisions. Grades in verbal or quantitative courses are used as a criterion of effectiveness for verbal or quantitative learning assistance to individuals. The assumption is that the individual's need to know in academic courses determines the questions he asks and thereby guides the support received, ensuring some relevance to the content of the academic program.

Level III decisions. Within an adjunct or follow-on academic course, the relationship between regular and developmental instruction and content is assessed. If the course grade is used as a criterion of the effectiveness of the developmental program, evaluators must decide whether the grade represents competencies developed in the remedial program.

Level IV decisions. The effectiveness of the relationship between the regular program and the developmental program is assessed. Evaluators decide whether entrance and exit standards are valid, recognized, and specific enough to guide instruction. A criterion for GPA is interpreted in light of the standards of achievement (i.e., competencies) represented by the grades from which GPA is derived.

Variable 26. Ongoing evaluation

Ongoing evaluation is associated with successful learning improvement programs (Grant and Hoeber 1978; Roueche and Snow 1977; Gordon 1975). Systematic evaluation and problem solving help to clarify institutional goals and programmatic objectives (Roueche and Snow 1977). Ongoing evaluation provides the basis for improving instructional services (Simmons et al. 1979; Maxwell 1975). Continuous assessment of needs and dissemination of information about the population to be served by the developmental program are necessary to build awareness, support, and rationale for instructional services. Ongoing evaluation facilitates awareness, negotiation, and innovation, which tend to produce not only better learning outcomes but also greater congruence between institutional philosophy and the working objectives for the program being evaluated.

A comprehensive evaluation of a learning improvement program should address several kinds of outcomes at various time

Systematic evaluation and problem solving help to clarify institutional goals and programmatic objectives.

intervals. Follow-up studies are an ongoing component of program assessment, addressing short-range goals, long-range goals, and carryover of skills to regular academic programs and requirements, and focusing on students who leave as well as those who complete the program (New York State Education Department 1977, pp. 73–74).

Level I decisions. No systematic evaluation of the effects of the remedial program on students' overall learning is undertaken.

Level II decisions. Evaluation is limited to a single semester.

Level III decisions. The effects of instructional services within a course and a related follow-on course are monitored.

Level IV decisions. Students' learning outcomes and needs are periodically assessed, and academic and developmental faculty receive regular feedback. Follow-up studies and analysis of long-term effects, trends, and changes are ongoing.

The structure of the remedial/developmental program as a facilitator of change

The development of an "innovative enclave" is a relatively inexpensive strategy for achieving institutional "self-renewal" and change (Levine 1978, p. 419). Collaboration to solve problems is an effective strategy for change, normally requiring a consultant in the role of "outside facilitator" (Nordvall 1982). The learning specialist fulfills the role of facilitator in successful learning improvement programs and uses the evaluation of needs and learning services as the starting point for problem solving.

The process of change involves four steps: (1) *research*, which uncovers possibilities and produces a theoretical basis for change; (2) *development*, which involves design of alternatives; (3) *diffusion*, which by dissemination and demonstration persuades target audiences to participate; and (4) *adoption*, which involves training, trial, installation, and institutionalization of the innovation (Stufflebeam 1971, p. 51).

Involvement of interdisciplinary faculty in the evaluation and redesign of instruction occurs naturally in those settings in which remedial/developmental services are being planned cooperatively for integration or have been integrated into ongoing academic programs. The central focus of the evaluation is the processes of the developmental program—their appropriateness given students' needs and the specific outcomes desired. Inevitably, the participating regular and developmental faculty analyze regular program processes as well, seeking information to help them refine their own course, program, or service. The ensuing analysis of a shared enterprise is unthreatening to participating faculty and affords evaluators much greater access and insight into regular programs than could otherwise be possible. Data thus obtained are more likely to explain more of the factors that would otherwise tend to confound the results in studies including only developmental processes.

An organizational structure that fosters joint projects and evaluations is therefore the critical element for the developmental program when the goal is evolutionary instructional change. Research has demonstrated that faculty's initiative and cooperation are essential if instructional development projects are to work and that faculty's initiative and cooperation are more important even than administrative and staff support (Lawrason and Hedberg 1977). What better way to foster such initiative and cooperation than to provide the possibility of alternatives and the faculty's involvement in the process of change?

The research literature provides strong support for three conclusions that, when ignored in the design of learning improvement programs and evaluation studies, produce programs with primarily short-term effects and studies that do not explain the basic instructional processes contributing to students' achievement.

1. In response to urgent pressures threatening academic values and survival, educators seek improved learning and retention in the overall academic program from their investment in remedial/developmental programs. These benefits have not been forthcoming from programs whose only service to the college is isolated remedial courses.

2. Instructional models for academic courses that are founded upon developmental learning theory and provide for all of the students' educational needs improve learning and are feasible and cost effective when developmental program resources are aligned with academic program resources.

3. The most effective roles for remedial/developmental programs in a college or university are those of catalyst and energizer for instructional development and of codeveloper, guide, and deliverer of services to create more responsive educational environments.

These generalizations can be expected to provide the most productive foundation for improved learning and academic program planning, as long as the current environment of declining population, diminished resources, and increasingly unethical competition for students prevails. The Decision Guide for Effective Programs is the pragmatic educator's blueprint for achieving survival with integrity and for controlling the processes of inevitable change.

BIBLIOGRAPHY

The ERIC Clearinghouse on Higher Education abstracts and indexes the current literature on higher education for the National Institute of Education's monthly bibliographic journal *Resources in Education.* Most of these publications are available through the ERIC Document Reproduction Service (EDRS). For publications cited in this bibliography that are available from EDRS, ordering number and price are included. Readers who wish to order a publication should write to the ERIC Document Reproduction Service, P.O. Box 190, Arlington, Virginia 22210. When ordering, please specify the document number. Documents are available as noted in microfiche (MF) and paper copy (PC). Since prices are subject to change it is advisable to check the latest issue of *Resources in Education* for current change based on the number of pages in the publication.

Adams, W. Royce. 1974. "The Reading Instructor's Role in Assisting Content Area Instructors in Reading and Study Skills." Paper presented at the annual meeting of the International Reading Association, New Orleans, Louisiana. ED 096 609. MF–$1.17; PC–$3.70.

American College Testing Program. 1980. *COMP: College Outcome Measures Project, Summary Report of Research and Development, 1976–1980.* Iowa City, Iowa: American College Testing Program.

Anderson, William W. 1973. "Evaluation of College Reading and Study Skills Programs: Problems and Approaches." Paper presented at the annual meeting of the College Reading Association, Silver Spring, Maryland. ED 084 514. MF–$1.17; PC–$3.70.

Arkwardy, Joseph W., and Chafin, Carl K. 1980. "The Transitional Curriculum Program: Toward Learner Independence through Developmental Education." Paper presented at the National Developmental Studies Conference, Atlanta, Georgia. ED 197 662. MF–$1.17; PC–$3.70.

Ashdown, E. March 1979. "Humanities on the Front Line." *Change* 11, 18–21.

Astin, Alexander W. 1975. *Preventing Students from Dropping Out.* San Francisco: Jossey-Bass.

Astin, H. S., et al. 1972. *Higher Education and the Disadvantaged Student.* Washington, D.C.: Human Services Press.

Baehr, R. F. 1969. "Project Success, Final Report." Washington, D.C.: Office of Education, DHEW. ED 039 870. MF–$1.17; PC–$7.20.

Baird, L. I. 1977. *Assessing Student Academic and Social Progress.* San Francisco: Jossey-Bass.

Ball, Samual. 1977. "Research and Program Evaluation: Some Principles, Precepts, and Practices." In *The Final Report of National Project II: Alternatives to the Revolving Door*, edited by R. A.

Donnovan. Washington, D.C.: Fund for the Improvement of Post-secondary Education. ED 151 054. MF–$1.17; PC–$3.70.

Barrow, John C. November 1980. "Follow-Up of Dropouts from Developmental Programs: A Supplemental Program Evaluation Approach." *Personnel and Guidance Journal* 59: 186–89.

Barshis, Don. 1979. "The Loop College Individual Needs (IN) Program: An Analysis of Its Success and a Guide to the Implementation or Adaptation of Its Techniques." Chicago: Loop College. ED 181 946. MF–$1.17; PC–$3.70.

Berg, E. H., and Axtell, D. 1968. Programs for Disadvantaged Students in California Community Colleges. Oakland: Peratta Junior College District. ED 026 032. MF–$1.17; PC–$9.33.

Bergman, Irwin B. January 1977. "Integrating Reading Skills with Content in a Two-Year College." *Journal of Reading* 20: 327–29.

Bernstein, H. R. 1976. *Manual for Teaching.* Ithaca, N.Y.: Center for Improvement of Undergraduate Education, Cornell University.

Bess, James L. May/June 1979. "Classroom and Management Decisions Using Student Data: Designing an Information System." *Journal of Higher Education* 50: 256–79.

Bliesmer, Emery P. 1956. "Review of Recent Research in College Reading." In *Exploring the Goals of College Reading Programs,* edited by O. S. Causey. Fort Worth: Texas Christian University Press. ED 130 222. MF–$1.17; PC–$3.70.

Boylan, Hunter. 1980. "Academic Intervention in Developmental Education." *Journal of Developmental and Remedial Education* 3:10–11.

———. 1981. "Program Evaluation: Issues, Needs, and Realities." In *Assessment of Learning Assistance Services,* edited by C. Walvekar. San Francisco: Jossey-Bass.

Braken, Dorothy K. 1954. "Organization and Administration of College Reading Programs: Problems Involved." In *Evaluating College Reading Programs,* edited by O. S. Causey. Fort Worth: Texas Christian University Press.

Brawer, Michael P. 1982. "Integrating Motivational Activities into Instruction: A Developmental Model." Tallahassee, Fla.: Department of Education. ED 222 106. MF–$1.17; PC–$3.70.

Brehman, George C., and McGowar, Kristine. 1976. "Higher Education Equal Opportunity Program: 1974–75. Annual Report." Harrisburg, Pa.: Pennsylvania Department of Education.

Bridge, W. T., ed. 1970. "Research and Compensatory Education: What Are We Doing?" Proceedings of a workshop sponsored by the Florida Educational Research Association, Jacksonville. ED 041 581. MF–$1.17; PC–$5.45.

Bronx Community College. 1974. "The Academic and Remedial Placement Profile of Students Entering B.C.C. in September 1974 by Curriculum Group." New York: Bronx Community College. ED 099 051. MF–$1.17; PC–$3.70.

———. 1975. "The Academic and Remedial Placement of Students Entering B.C.C. in September 1975 by Curriculum Group." New York: Bronx Community College. ED 115 330. MF–$1.17; PC–$3.70.

Bruner, Jerome. 1973. *The Relevance of Education.* New York: Norton Library.

Bynum, Effie, et al. 1972. *Report of the Study of College Compensatory Education Programs for Disadvantaged Youth: A Draft.* New York: Columbia University Teachers College. ED 110 525. MF–$1.37; PC–$39.26.

Carnegie Council on Policy Studies in Higher Education. 1979. *Fair Practices in Higher Education.* San Francisco: Jossey-Bass.

———. 1980. *Three Thousand Futures: The Next Twenty Years for Higher Education.* San Francisco: Jossey-Bass. ED 183 076. MF–$1.17; PC not available EDRS.

Carnegie Foundation for the Advancement of Teaching. 1977. *Missions of the College Curriculum.* San Francisco: Jossey-Bass.

Carney, Myrna, and Geis, Lynna. 1981. "Reading Ability, Academic Performance, and College Attrition." *Journal of College Student Personnel* 22: 55–59.

Carter, Homer. 1970. "The Impact of Today's Students upon College Programs in Reading." Paper presented at the national conference of the International Reading Association, St. Petersburg, Florida. ED 049 004. MF–$1.17; PC–$3.70.

Carter, Larry G. 1976. "Developmental Studies Project: Post Secondary Education: Final Report." Canandaigua, N.Y.: Community College of the Finger Lakes. ED 131 888. MF–$1.17; PC–$5.45.

Causey, Oscar S., ed. 1955. *What the Colleges Are Doing in Planning and Improving College Reading Programs.* Fort Worth: Texas Christian University Press. ED 130 220. MF–$1.17; PC–$14.97.

———. 1956. *Exploring the Goals of College Reading Programs.* Fort Worth: Texas Christian University Press. ED 130 222. MF–$1.17; PC–$12.83.

———. 1957. *Significant Elements in College and Adult Reading Improvement.* Fort Worth: Texas Christian University Press. ED 130 223. MF–$1.17; PC–$12.83.

Chaplin, Miriam T. May 1977a. "An Analysis of Current Procedures, Practices, and Principles in College Reading Instruction." *Reading World* 16: 270–78.

———. 1977b. "Where Do We Go from Here? Strategies for Survival of College Reading Programs." Paper presented to the annual meeting of the College Reading Association, Cincinnati, Ohio. ED 147 791. MF–$1.17; PC–$3.70.

Chickering, Arthur W. 1969. *Education and Identity*. San Francisco: Jossey-Bass.

Christensin, F. A. 1971. "The Development of an Academic System for Educationally Disadvantaged Students." Paper presented at the APGA meeting, Atlantic City. ED 050 211. MF–$1.17; PC–$3.70.

Chronicle of Higher Education. 16 December 1981. "Academic Norms Urged for Aid Recipients." 23: 16–17.

Cohen, Arthur M. April 1979. "Shall We Segregate the Functionally Illiterate?" *Community and Junior College Journal* 49: 14–18.

Cole, Charles C., Jr., 1982. *Improving Instruction: Issues and Alternatives for Higher Education*. AAHE-ERIC/Higher Education Research Report No. 4. Washington, D.C.: American Association for Higher Education. ED 222 159. MF–$1.17; PC–$7.20.

Cross, K. Patricia. 1976. *Accent on Learning*. San Francisco: Jossey-Bass.

————. 1979. "Looking Ahead: Spotlight on the Learner." Paper presented at the National Conference on Developmental Education, Lexington, Kentucky. ED 177 971. MF–$1.17; PC–$3.70.

————. 1981. *Adults as Learners*. San Francisco: Jossey-Bass.

David, J. L., and Pelavin, S. H. 1978. "Secondary Analysis in Compensatory Education Programs." In *Secondary Analysis*, edited by R. F. Barouch. New Directions for Testing and Measurement No. 4. San Francisco: Jossey-Bass.

Davis, J. A., et al. 1973. "The Impact of Special Services Programs in Higher Education for Disadvantaged Students." Princeton, N.J.: Educational Testing Service.

Diamond, Lynn. 1976. "The Development of Reading Skills through a Holistic Team Teaching Approach." Paper presented at the annual meeting of the International Reading Association, Anaheim, California. ED 123 579. MF–$1.17; PC–$3.70.

Donnovan, Richard A., ed. 1977. *The Final Report of National Project II: Alternatives to the Revolving Door*. Washington, D.C.: Fund for the Improvement of Postsecondary Education. ED 151 054. MF–$1.17; PC–$9.33.

Duck, Gary A. 1978. *Student Performance Measures for Evaluating Secondary and Postsecondary Intervention Programs*, vol. 5 of *Planned Variations Study*. Washington, D.C.: Office of Education. ED 154 674. MF–$1.17; PC–$11.08.

Eagle, Norman. 1977. "The Academic and Remedial Placement Profile of Students Entering B.C.C. in September 1976 and September 1977 by Curriculum Group." Research Report BCC 4-76, 4-77. New York: Bronx Community College. ED 148 434. MF–$1.17; PC–$7.20.

Educational Testing Service. 1981. *National Report on College-Bound Seniors, 1981*. Princeton, N.J.: ETS.

Entwisle, D. R. March 1960. "Evaluations of Study-Skills Courses: A Review." *Journal of Educational Research* 53:243–51.

Fairbanks, Marilyn M., and Snozek, Dorothy A. 1973. "Checklist of Current Practices in Reading and Study Skills Programs for College Students." Paper presented at the annual meeting of the College Reading Association, Silver Spring, Maryland. ED 088 020. MF–$1.17; PC–$3.70.

Fincher, Cameron. 1975. "The Access Placement Retention Graduation of Minority Students in Higher Education." Paper presented at a conference on equality of access in postsecondary education, Atlanta, Georgia. ED 114 011. MF–$1.17; PC–$7.20.

Fishman, F., and Dugan, M. 1976. "Alternative Programs and Services for the Non-Traditional Student." Philadelphia: Community College. ED 129 380. MF–$1.17; PC–$3.70.

Flippo, Rona F. 1980. "The Need for Comparison Studies of College Students' Reading Gains in Developmental Programs Using General and Specific Levels of Diagnosis." Paper presented at the Southeastern Regional Conference of the International Reading Association, Nashville, Tennessee. ED 185 525. MF–$1.17; PC–$3.70.

Glasser, William, M. D. 1969. *Schools without Failure*. New York: Harper & Row.

Gordon, Edmund W. 1975. *Opportunity Programs for the Disadvantaged in Higher Education*. AAHE-ERIC/Higher Education Research Report No. 6. Washington, D.C.: American Association for Higher Education. ED 114 028. MF–$1.17; PC–$3.70.

Gordon, Edmund W., and Wilkerson, Doxey. 1966. *Compensatory Education for the Disadvantaged*. New York: College Entrance Examination Board. ED 011 274. MF–$1.17; PC–$26.24.

Grant, Gerald, et al. 1979. *On Competence: A Critical Analysis of Competence-Based Reforms in Higher Education*. San Francisco: Jossey-Bass.

Grant, Mary K., and Hoeber, Daniel R. 1978. *Basic Skills Programs: Are They Working?* AAHE-ERIC/Higher Education Research Report No. 1. Washington, D.C.: American Association for Higher Education. ED 150 918. MF–$1.17; PC–$7.20.

Holmberg, James, et al. 1979. *The Teaching of History to Developmental Students: A Block Project*. Pittsburgh: Allegheny County Community College. ED 168 617. MF–$1.17; PC–$5.45.

Jason, Emil, et al. 1976. "Accelerated Program in Mathematics for Disadvantaged Students." Paper presented at the TBIO Programs Conference, Fontanno, Wisconsin. ED 152 931. MF–$1.17; PC–$5.45.

Jelfo, Donald T. 1974. *An Evaluation of the Developmental Education Program at Cuyahoga Community College*. Fort Lauderdale, Fla.: Nova University. ED 099 036. MF–$1.17; PC–$3.70.

Kagan, Jerome. 25 February 1973. "The Deprived Child: Doomed To Be Retarded?" *Los Angeles Times*.

Kahn, Edward. 1977. "A Survey of Community College Reading Programs and Personnel in New Jersey." Master's thesis, Rutgers University. ED 150 557. MF–$1.17; PC–$14.97.

Keimig, Ruth Talbott. 1982. "The Change Facilitator Model for Managing and Evaluating Developmental Studies Programs Applied to the Study of Freshmen Achievement and Persistence at the Marymount College of Virginia." Ed.D. dissertation, George Washington University.

Kendrick, S. A. 1969. "Extending Educational Opportunity: Problems of Recruitment and Admissions, High Risk Students." Summary of a paper presented at the 55th Annual Meeting of the Association of American Colleges, Pittsburgh, Pennsylvania. ED 025 227. MF–$1.17; PC–$3.70.

Kettlewell, Gail B. 1978. "All College Students Benefit from Reading Instruction." Paper presented to the annual meeting of the Southeastern Conference on English in the Two-Year Colleges, Nashville, Tennessee. ED 159 622. MF–$1.17; PC–$3.70.

Killian, C. Rodney, ed. 1980. *Reasoning, Piaget, and Higher Education*. Papers presented at the National Conference of Reasoning, Piaget, and Higher Education, Denver, Colorado. ED 197 644. MF–$1.17; PC–$11.08.

Kingston, Albert J. 1955. "Problems in the Administration of a College Reading Program." In *What the Colleges Are Doing in Planning and Improving College Reading Programs*, edited by O. S. Causey. Fort Worth: Texas Christian University Press. ED 130 220. MF–$1.17; PC–$14.97.

Klingelhofer, Edwin L., and Hollander, Lynne. 1973. *Educational Characteristics and Needs of New Students: A Review of the Literature*. 2d ed. Berkeley: Center for Research and Development in Higher Education. ED 084 482. MF–$1.17; PC–$14.97.

Lawrason, Robin E., and Hedberg, John G. 1977. "Predicting Successful Instructional Development Projects in Higher Education." Paper presented at a meeting of the American Educational Research Association. ED 153 555. MF–$1.17; PC–$5.45.

Lesnick, M. 1972. "Reading and Study Behavior Problems of College Freshmen." *Reading World* 296–319.

Levine, Arthur. 1978. *Handbook on Undergraduate Curriculum*. San Francisco: Jossey-Bass.

———. 1980. *When Dreams and Heroes Died: A Portrait of Today's College Student*. San Francisco: Jossey-Bass.

Losak, J., and Burns, N. 1971. "An Evaluation of the Community College Studies Program for the Year 1969–70." Miami: Miami-Dade Junior College. ED 056 683. MF–$1.17; PC–$11.08.

Ludwig, L. Mark. 1977. *Educational Consulting Study: Special Techniques for Assisting the Underprepared College Student*. Working Papers on Professional Development in Teaching No. 5. Cleveland: Cleveland Commission on Higher Education. ED 175 324. MF–$1.17; PC–$5.45.

McAllister, David. 1954. "Enlisting Faculty Aid." In *Evaluating College Reading Programs*, edited by O. S. Causey. Fort Worth: Texas Christian University Press. ED 130 221. MF–$1.17; PC–$3.70.

McCabe, Robert H. May 1981. "Now Is the Time to Reform the American Community College." *Community and Junior College Journal* 51: 6–10.

McDill, et al. 1969. *Strategies for Success in Compensatory Education*. Baltimore: Johns Hopkins Press.

McFadden, Ronald. 1979. "Program Evaluation and Educational Research in Developmental Studies: A Systems Model." Athens, Ga.: University of Georgia. ED 184 393. MF–$1.17; PC–$5.45.

Magarrell, J. 10 March 1980. "Use Tests of Students to Judge Performance of Colleges, Ex-Education Commissioner Urges." *Chronicle of Higher Education*, 22:8.

———. 1 June 1981. "Colleges Offered 15 Percent More Courses This Year, Survey Finds; Remedial Classes Increase 22 Percent." *Chronicle of Higher Education*. 23: 173.

Manzo, Anthony. 1979. "College Reading: Clone, Illegitimate Child, or Hybrid?" ED 178 881. MF–$1.17; PC–$3.70.

Maxwell, Martha. 1970. "Evaluation of College Reading and Study Skills Programs." Paper presented at the conference of the International Reading Association, Anaheim, California. ED 045 294. MF–$1.17; PC–$3.70.

———. March 1975. "Developing a Learning Center: Plans, Problems, Progress." *Journal of Reading* 18: 462–69.

———. 1979. *Improving Student Learning Skills*. San Francisco: Jossey-Bass.

Mayhew, Lewis B. 1979. *Surviving the Eighties*. San Francisco: Jossey-Bass.

Meister, M., et al. October 1962. "Operation Second Chance." *Junior College Journal* 33: 78–88.

Minnick, Kirk F., and Teitelbaum, Herta. 1980. "Impact of a Developmental Program on Student Performance." Paper presented at the annual forum of the Association for Institutional Research, Atlanta, Georgia. ED 189 938. MF–$1.17; PC–$5.45.

Moore, Robert L. 1981. "Role and Scope of Evaluation." In *Assessment of Learning Assistance Services*, edited by C. Walvekar. San Francisco: Jossey-Bass.

Moran, Patrick J. 1980. "Piggybacking Reading and Study Skills onto College Courses." Paper presented at the annual meeting of the International Reading Association, St. Louis, Missouri. ED 186 879. MF–$1.17; PC–$3.70.

Mornell, Eugene S. 1973. "The Program of Special Directed Studies: A Five-Year Summary." Claremont, Calif.: Claremont University Center. ED 088 638. MF–$1.17; PC–$3.70.

Newsweek. 8 December 1975 "Why Johnny Can't Write." 58–61.

Newton, Eunice S. 1982. *The Case for Improved College Learning: Instructing High Risk Students.* New York: Vantage Press.

New York State Education Department. 1977. *Developmental Studies for Occupational Students: Postsecondary Programs.* Albany: New York State Education Department. ED 173 635. MF–$1.17; PC–$12.83.

———. 1980. *New York State Programs of Postsecondary Opportunity, 1977–78 and 1978–79.* Albany: New York State Education Department. ED 197 030. MF–$1.17; PC–$9.33.

Nordvall, Robert C. 1982. *The Process of Change in Higher Education Institutions.* AAHE-ERIC/Higher Education Research Report No. 7. Washington, D.C.: American Association for Higher Education. HE 015 832. MF–$1.17; PC–$7.20.

Obler, Martin, et al. January/February 1977. "Combining Traditional Counseling, Instruction, and Mentoring Functions with Academically Deficient College Freshmen." *Journal of Educational Research* 70: 142–47.

Ozer, Mark N. 1980. *Solving Learning and Behavior Problems of Children.* San Francisco: Jossey-Bass.

Pedrini, Bonnie C., and Pedrini, D. T. 1970. "Reading Ability and Grades: A Brief Review." Omaha: University of Nebraska at Omaha. ED 087 510. MF–$1.17; PC–$3.70.

Pinette, Clayton, and Smith, Kent, eds. 1979. *College Reading Skills.* Newark, Del.: International Reading Association. ED 179 915. MF–$1.17; PC–$5.45.

Renner, S. M. 1979. "College Reading Programs: What Is Success?" In *College Reading Skills*, edited by Clayton Pinette and Kent Smith. Newark, Del.: International Reading Association. ED 179 915. MF–$1.17; PC–$5.45.

Richardson, Richard C., Jr., et al. 1981. *Functional Literacy in the College Setting.* AAHE-ERIC/Higher Education Research Report No. 3. Washington, D.C.: American Association for Higher Education. ED 211 032. MF–$1.17; PC–$7.20.

Robinson, H. Alan. 1965. "Critique of Current Research in College and Adult Reading." In *New Concepts in College-Adult Reading*, edited by E. L. Thruston. New Orleans, La.: National Reading Conference. ED 176 244. MF–$1.17; PC–$3.70.

Rossman, J. E., Astin, A. W., et al. 1975. *Open Admissions at the City University of New York: An Analysis of the First Year.* Englewood Cliffs, N.J.: Prentice Hall.

Roueche, John E. 1981–82. "Don't Close the Door." *Community and Junior College Journal* 52: 17–23.

Roueche, John E., and Kirk, R. Wade. 1973. *Catching Up: Remedial Education*. San Francisco: Jossey-Bass.

Roueche, John E., and Snow, Jerry J. 1977. *Overcoming Learning Problems*. San Francisco: Jossey-Bass.

Sadler, William A., Jr., and Whimbey, Arthur. 1979. "Developing a Cognitive Skills Approach to Teaching." Paper presented at a conference of the American Association of Higher Education, Washington, D.C. ED 187 380. MF–$1.17; PC–$3.70.

Sanders, Vickie. 1980. "College Reading and Study Programs: Do They Make Any Difference?" Paper presented at the annual meeting of the Western College Reading Association, San Francisco, California. ED 185 532. MF–$1.17; PC–$3.70.

Schiavone, J. Summer 1977. "Integrated Remediation for the Community College." *Improving College and University Teaching* 24: 183–85.

Shaughnessy, Mina P. 1977. *Errors and Expectations: A Guide for the Teacher of Basic Writing*. New York: Oxford University Press.

Shaw, Phillip B. 1960. "Integration of Reading Instruction with Regular Offerings." In *Phases of College and Other Adult Reading Programs*, edited by E. P. Bliesmer. Fort Worth: National Reading Conference, Inc. ED 176 251. MF–$1.17; PC–$3.70.

Sherman, Robert H., and Tinto, Vincent. 1975. "The Effectiveness of Secondary and Higher Education Intervention Programs: A Critical Review of Research." Paper presented at the annual meeting of the American Educational Research Association, Washington, D.C. ED 106 378. MF–$1.17; PC–$5.45.

Simmons, Ron, et al. 1979. "Teaching the Disadvantaged in Engineering." ED 180 356. MF–$1.17; PC–$7.20.

Slack, Warner V., and Porter, Douglas. May 1980. "The Scholastic Aptitude Test: A Critical Appraisal." *Harvard Educational Review* 50: 154–75.

Smith, G. M. 1972. "The Two-Year Compensatory Program of the College of Basic Studies: Implications of a Successful Model." In *On Equality of Educational Opportunity*, edited by F. Mosteller and D. P. Moynihan. New York: Vintage.

Sparks, June R., and Davis, Cynthia L. 1977. "A Systems Analysis and Evaluation of a Junior College Developmental Studies Program." Paper presented at the annual meeting of the American Educational Research Association, New York, New York. ED 136 892. MF–$1.17; PC–$3.70.

tufflebeam, D. I. 1971. *Educational Evaluation and Decision Making*. Itasca, Ill.: F. E. Peacock Publishers.

illman, Chester E. Spring 1973. "Four-Year College Reading Programs and Grades: An Annotated Review, 1945–1971." *Journal of Reading Behavior* 100–109.

Trillin, Alice S., and Associates. 1980. *Teaching Basic Skills in College*. San Francisco: Jossey-Bass.

Walter, Judith M. 1979. "The Emergent Role of Reading Specialists as Consultants to College Faculties." In *College Reading Skills*, edited by C. Pinette and K. Smith. Newark, Del.: International Reading Association. ED 179 915. MF–$1.17; PC–$3.70.

Walvekar, Carol C., ed. 1981. *Assessment of Learning Assistance Services*. San Francisco: Jossey-Bass.

Wassman, Rose. 1977. *California College Reading Programs: The State of the State*. De Anza College, California. ED 146 559. MF–$1.17; PC–$3.70.

Watkins, Beverly T. 2 February 1981. "Scholars Increasingly Concerned about Deterioration of Literacy." *Chronicle of Higher Education* 23:1.

Webb, Jeanine. 1977. "Program Evaluation: Cognitive Achievement." In *The Final Report of National Project II: Alternatives to the Revolving Door*, edited by R. A. Donnovan. Washington, D.C.: Fund for the Improvement of Postsecondary Education. ED 151 054. MF–$1.17; PC–$7.20.

Wellborn, S. N. 20 October 1980. "Cheating in College Becomes an Epidemic." *U.S. News and World Report* 39–42.

Whimbey, Arthur, and Lockhead, J. 1981. *Problem Solving and Comprehension: A Short Course in Analytical Reasoning*. 2d ed. Philadelphia: The Franklin Institute.

ASHE-ERIC HIGHER EDUCATION RESEARCH REPORTS

Starting in 1983 the Association for the Study of Higher Education assumed co-sponsorship of the Higher Education Research Reports with the ERIC Clearinghouse on Higher Education. For the previous 11 years ERIC and the American Association for Higher Education prepared and published the reports.

Each report is the definitive analysis of a tough higher education problem, based on a thorough research of pertinent literature and institutional experiences. Report topics, identified by a national survey, are written by noted practitioners and scholars with prepublication manuscript reviews by experts.

Ten monographs in the ASHE-ERIC/Higher Education Research Report series are published each year, available individually or by subscription. Subscription to 10 issues is $50 regular; $35 for members of AERA, AAHE, and AIR; $30 for members of ASHE. (Add $7.50 outside U.S.)

Prices for single copies, including 4th class postage and handling, are $6.50 regular and $5.00 for members of AERA, AAHE, AIR, and ASHE. If faster first-class postage is desired for U.S. and Canadian orders, add $.60; for overseas, add $4.50. For VISA and MasterCard payments, give card number, expiration date, and signature. Orders under $25 must be prepaid. Bulk discounts are available on orders of 25 or more of a single title. Order from the Publications Department, Association for the Study of Higher Education, One Dupont Circle, Suite 630, Washington, D.C. 20036, (202) 296-2597. Write for a complete list of Higher Education Research Reports and other ASHE and ERIC publications.

1981 Higher Education Research Reports

1. Minority Access to Higher Education
   Jean L. Preer

2. Institutional Advancement Strategies in Hard Times
   Michael D. Richards and Gerald Sherratt

3. Functional Literacy in the College Setting
   Richard C. Richardson, Jr., Kathryn J. Martens, and Elizabeth C. Fisk

4. Indices of Quality in the Undergraduate Experience
   George D. Kuh

5. Marketing in Higher Education
   Stanley M. Grabowski

6. Computer Literacy in Higher Education
   Francis E. Masat

7. Financial Analysis for Academic Units
   Donald L. Walters

   Assessing the Impact of Faculty Collective Bargaining
   J. Victor Baldridge, Frank K. Kemerer, and Associates

9. Strategic Planning, Management, and Decision Making
   Robert G. Cope

10. Organizational Communication in Higher Education
    Robert D. Gratz and Philip J. Salem

1982 Higher Education Research Reports

1. Rating College Teaching: Criterion Studies of Student Evaluation-of-Instruction Instruments
   Sidney E. Benton

2. Faculty Evaluation: The Use of Explicit Criteria for Promotion, Retention, and Tenure
   Neal Whitman and Elaine Weiss

3. The Enrollment Crisis: Factors, Actors, and Impacts
   J. Victor Baldridge, Frank R. Kemerer, and Kenneth C. Green

4. Improving Instruction: Issues and Alternatives for Higher Education
   Charles C. Cole, Jr.

5. Planning for Program Discontinuance: From Default to Design
   Gerlinda S. Melchiori

6. State Planning, Budgeting, and Accountability: Approaches for Higher Education
   Carol E. Floyd

7. The Process of Change in Higher Education Institutions
   Robert C. Nordvall

8. Information Systems and Technological Decisions: A Guide for Non-Technical Administrators
   Robert L. Bailey

9. Government Support for Minority Participation in Higher Education
   Kenneth C. Green

10. The Department Chair: Professional Development and Role Conflict
    David B. Booth

1983 Higher Education Research Reports

1. The Path to Excellence: Quality Assurance in Higher Education
   Laurence R. Marcus, Anita O. Leone, and Edward D. Goldberg

2. Faculty Recruitment, Retention, and Fair Employment: Obligations and Opportunities
   John S. Waggaman

3. The Crisis in Faculty Careers: Changes and Challenges
   Michael C. T. Brookes and Katherine L. German